ABt

25 Bicycle Tours in Southern Indiana

✓

25 Bicycle Tours in Southern Indiana

Scenic and Historic Rides through Hoosier Country

Chuck Fearnow, John Kistler, and J. Edward Pope

A 25 Bicycle Tours™ Book
Backcountry Publications
Countryman Press, Inc.
Woodstock, Vermont

An Invitation to the Reader— Although it is unlikely that the roads you cycle on these tours will change much with time, some road signs, landmarks, and other items may. If you find that changes have occurred on these routes, please let us know so we may correct them in future editions. Address all correspondence to:

Editor
25 Bicycle Tours™ Series
Backcountry Publications
PO Box 175
Woodstock, VT 05091

Allen County Public Library
900 Webster Street
PO Box 2270
Fort Wayne, IN 46801-2270

Library of Congress Cataloging-in-Publication Data

Fearnow, Chuck, 1946
   25 bicycle tours in southern Indiana: scenic and historic rides through Hoosier country / Chuck Fearnow, John Kistler, and J. Edward Pope.
      p.   cm.—(A 25 bicycle tours book)
   ISBN 0-88150-232-4
   1. Bicycle touring—Indiana—Guidebooks. 2. Indiana—Description and travel—1981- I. Kistler, John, 1954- . II. Pope, J. Edward, 1956- . III. Title. IV. Title: Twenty-five bicycle tours in southern Indiana. V. Series.
GV1045.5.I6F4   1992
796.6'4'09772—dc20   92-15833
                                                                              CIP

Published by Backcountry Publications
A division of The Countryman Press, Inc.
Woodstock, Vermont 05091

Printed in the United States of America
Text and cover design by Richard Widhu
Cover photo by Barbara Fearnow
Photos by the Authors
Maps by Richard Widhu, © 1992 Backcountry Publications

Acknowledgments

The joy of cycling is the trip you take, the experiences and adventures you have and the people you meet. In that respect, then we have had a wonderful adventure in writing this book, because we have had the good fortune to meet some very nice, helpful people. People like our publisher Carl Taylor, who encouraged us and never lost his faith, our editors Robin Dutcher-Bayer who worried about us, and never lost her composure and Janet Biehl who dotted all the "i's" and crossed the "t's" without fail. We have been fortunate to know them, and we all want to thank them. There are others we would like to thank individually as well.

Ed Pope would like to thank: "Terre Haute" Bob Tyron who helped scout the routes through Spring Mill, Evansville, New Harmony, and also supplied a great deal of information (and misinformation) about Terre Haute—he even shared his prime rib at Jack's Lounge in Mitchell; his mother Irene Pope, for her assistance in scouting the rides through Nashville and Columbus; Dave Duclos, who helped scout the ride through Oldenburg; the guys at The Sampler, for their route suggestions in Rush County; Mark and Marlene Porter, who supplied most of the route through the New Harmony area; Kim Tepool, from the Evansville Convention and Visitor's Bureau, for her route suggestions in the Evansville area; Fran Abbot, from the Linton-Stockton Chamber of Commerce, for information on Linton and Bruce Borders, the Elvis impersonator, and mayor of Jacksonville.

John Kistler would like to give special thanks to his wife, Martha, and daughter, Erin, for all their love and encouragement. Thanks to Tim "Julio" Wall, Jay Ellis, Mark Green, and Alex Black for sharing and creating so many great times.

Chuck Fearnow would like to give his deeply felt thanks to Barbara and Jonathan for their help and patience, and the many Hoosiers who have added to the pleasure of riding in Indiana.

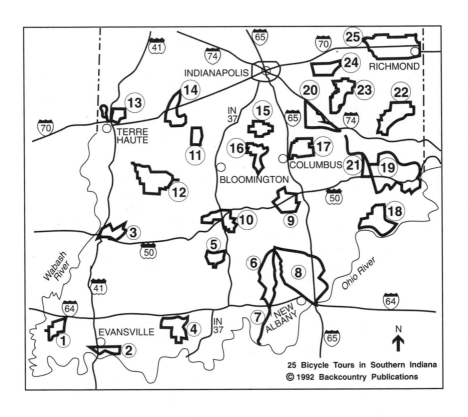
25 Bicycle Tours in Southern Indiana
© 1992 Backcountry Publications

Contents

Introduction

Rivers, forests, plains, and hills combine in Indiana in unique land formations. The early mix of fur traders and pioneers who came overland from the north and northeast and upriver from the south formed a singular mixture of cultures, philosophies, and histories. Southern Indiana blends all of these into a distinctive and exciting cycling experience through Indiana, the home of Hoosiers.

Hoosiers

There are a variety of stories about what the word *Hoosier* means, most of which don't seem very plausible. The one I like best, and the one you are going to hear first, is about a man named Samuel Hoosier. Hoosier, a Kentuckian, had a reputation for hiring honest workers from the Indiana side of the Ohio River. Soon these honest workers came to be known as Hoosiers, and later everyone on the Indiana side was known as a Hoosier.

James Whitcomb Riley, the famous late-nineteenth-century Hoosier poet, had a different story. He said that the name *Hoosier* came from "a settler who came into a barroom on a morning after a fight, and seeing an ear on the floor, would merely push it aside with his foot and carelessly ask, 'Whose ear?'"

A lot of Hoosiers are farmers. When you're cycling through the countryside, many of the people you meet will be farmers, or merchants who serve farmers. People who live in the small towns aren't farmers, but they think and act like farmers. Indiana farmers are a hard-working, honest, friendly, polite, conservative people, and they tend to like people who are like them. They generally have little use for people who are too faddish or quick-talking. You probably will never meet a fast-talking Hoosier farmer wearing the latest style.

When I was a boy wandering Indiana with my folks or grandparents, I spent a lot of time in the farm country. Anytime we drove onto a secondary blacktop or gravel road, we would be greeted by the driver of every car that passed us going the other direction. They used to use the Sterling Moss wave. One hand is extended into the air briefly and then brought back down—the way Sterling Moss used to do when he was racing. Sometimes there would be a slight cocking of the hand backward and a slow release forward as a variation on this wave, but usually not. Many Hoosier farmers consider this much too demonstrative and don't use it.

Today, Hoosier farmers still wave to everyone they pass, but over the last ten to twenty years, the Sterling Moss wave has lost popularity to the "microwave." A microwave is given by extending the index finger momentarily. The driver of a vehicle usually drives with his right hand on top of the steering wheel. As you approach, he will extend his index finger as a greeting. This is a proper greeting and is not an insult at all. The proper response to this greeting is either a return microwave, a Sterling Moss wave, or a nod of the head. The chin should not dip more than a half-inch in this nod.

The microwave will probably still be popular after another ten or twenty years—Hoosiers aren't faddish. When you are traveling down a country road, you can tell the locals from the foreigners as easily as if they were wearing a sign-anyone who doesn't give you a microwave is a foreigner.

The kind of people you will meet in the country in Indiana are friendly, but they are not overly warm. They are polite, but not overly talkative. They are honest to a fault and slow to change. Hoosiers in the big cities are a mixture of this type of person and big-city people anywhere. Some city Hoosiers are exactly like the farmers, while others have acquired the best qualities of farmers and adapted them as well as can be expected to city life. They are honest, sincere people who go about their business, leave other people alone, and are polite. Unfortunately, some city folk have acquired the worst qualities of farmers and combined them with the worst qualities of city folk. These people seem to have little respect for anyone, like some big-city people, and resist change like farmers. They lack the deeply ingrained honesty of farmers, and they are usually in a big-city hurry to do something important, like go home to watch TV. They are a nuisance and often obtain political jobs, where they can annoy large numbers of people.

Hoosier History

Wandering Indians were the first human inhabitants of Indiana. The burial mounds that they built can still be seen throughout the state. The wandering Indians were replaced by farming Indians, who were then replaced by warlike hunting tribes approximately one hundred years before the Europeans arrived. The Miami, Pottawattomi, Delaware, and Shawnee tribes were the chief occupants of Indiana when the French arrived.

The French explorer Robert Cavalier de La Salle, was the first European to set foot in Indiana, in 1679. By 1732, the French had already established trading posts at Lafayette, Fort Wayne, and Vincennes. The British took this area in 1763, after they defeated France in the French and Indian War (1689-1763). The British government immediately forbade any colonial settlements west of the Appalachian Mountains, reserving the Great Lakes and the Ohio River valley for the Indians. Explorers like Daniel Boone ignored this proclamation, and soon small communities were established in present-day Ohio and Kentucky.

Overlooking the Ohio River in Madison, IN

The daring exploits of George Rogers Clark during the Revolutionary War won the Ohio River valley for the United States. The area was called the Northwest Territory and was claimed by several states. To settle the disputes, Congress enacted the Ordinance of 1787, which defined methods of surveying and selling the land and set requirements for the territory's organization and application for statehood. In 1800 the Indiana Territory was separated from the Northwest Territory. It was made up of part or all of present-day Indiana, Illinois, Michigan, Wisconsin, and Minnesota, with the capital being in Vincennes. William Henry Harrison was governor of the Indiana Territory.

The Indiana Territory was the last place where the Indians had a chance to stop the westward migration of settlers. In 1811, Harrison defeated Tecumseh and his brother The Prophet at the Battle of Tippecanoe near Lafayette and destroyed the powerful confederation of Indian tribes that Tecumseh, a Shawnee chief, had been trying to organize. Tecumseh was killed a short time later in a battle with Harrison near Detroit. The Indiana Territory was reduced to the present state borders in 1812.

In 1813 the territorial government was moved to Corydon. Two years later, the territorial legislature petitioned Congress to grant Indiana statehood. A state constitutional convention was held in June 1816 to draft Indiana's first constitution, and Indiana was admitted to the Union on December 11, 1816. At that time the state was still two-thirds wilderness, and over half of it was still owned by the Indians. The first state constitution was a progressive document that granted a free public education through college to all citizens of the state. This noble gesture never became a reality, as the state could not implement the idea before it was deleted in the state's second constitution in 1851.

To encourage more rapid settlement, the state capital was moved to a centralized site, Indianapolis, in 1825. Two years later, construction began on the National Road and the Michigan Road. The National Road brought settlers from Ohio, Pennsylvania and other points north and east. The Michigan Road, the Ohio River, the Whitewater River, and the Wabash River brought settlers from Kentucky, Tennessee, and points south. As settlers poured into the state, demands for more transportation facilities caused the legislature to adopt the Mammoth Internal Improvement Act of 1836. Thirteen million dollars in bonds were sold in order to build a series of canals, railroads, and roads throughout the state. At the time, the state had an annual budget of only $60,000. Indiana was not alone in having this type of internal improvement mania. By 1840, Ohio and Michigan had both gone bankrupt trying to do the same thing. Indiana was supposed to go bankrupt in 1838, but the state legislature offered to pay a pittance for the bonds; the debtors accepted, and Indiana avoided the legal confines of bankruptcy.

In 1851, a second (the present) state constitution was written. Because of the financial fiasco created by the Mammoth Internal Improvements Act, this constitution forbade the state to go into debt. Also by 1851, all the Indian tribes had relinquished their claims to land, and only a few hundred were still living in the state.

During the Civil War, Indiana was Lincoln's strongest supporter, sending more than 200,000 men into battle. Perhaps Hoosiers felt a special tie to Lincoln because he had grown up in Indiana, or perhaps they were influenced by the Quakers, who had been running underground railroads for years before the war; perhaps it was a little of both. Either way, more than 24,000 Hoosiers lost their lives, still the largest number of Hoosiers to die in any war. However, only one battle was fought in Indiana—a raid by 2,500 Confederate cavalrymen led by General John Hunt Morgan.

After the Civil War, the railroads' expansion led to new industry and growth in the cities. By 1900, Indiana had shifted from an agricultural state to an urban industrial state. Eugene Debs of Terre Haute was one of the early labor organizers, and he was imprisoned for a short time for his activities. After serving time in the "big house," Debs tried to get time in the White House but was unsuccessful.

During the 1920s the Ku Klux Klan was the dominant political force in Indiana. The KKK's dominance ended when the head of the KKK was imprisoned for murder.

Because Indiana was so heavily industrialized, the Great Depression hurt Indiana more than many other states. The state was further swamped by the Ohio River flood of 1937, which caused $500 million in damage.

During the last fifty years, Indiana's economic growth has largely been tied to the automotive and steel industries of its northern and central regions. These industries brought prosperity for many years, then declined; the economy is now relatively stable. Agriculture has shifted from small farms to large efficient businesses. Much of Indiana's current economy is based in industry and agriculture, but services have gained a stronghold and are growing.

Indiana remains a hybrid of industry, agriculture, and service; of southern and northern; of conservative and liberal. The pendulum slowly swings from one to the other, depending on the time and place.

Hoosier Geology

Three broad east-west bands (see map) make up Indiana's basic geology. The middle one, the Tipton Till Plain, is the one most people think of when they visualize Indiana. The Tipton Till Plain crosses the state roughly from Fort Wayne to just south of Indianapolis. This middle band is mostly flat, except for rivers and creeks. Looking out over it is much like looking out over the ocean-except in August, when, of course, the corn is too high to see over.

The northern band is a moraine and lake region that was formed mostly by glacial erosion. Most notable in the northwestern area are the spectacular sand dunes on Lake Michigan at the Indiana Dunes State Park, but also interesting are the peat bogs, kettle holes, kames, and lakes. The northeastern portion of the northern band is filled with rolling hills, and numerous small natural lakes.

The southern band, where the tours in this book are located, is geographically more diverse. Seven north-south strips divide this band in a roller coaster of ups and downs. This area has great topographic relief, especially around the rivers and creeks. The highest elevation in the state is just north of Richmond, in the Dearborn Upland on the eastern border of Indiana, while the lowest point is also in this southern region-the Ohio River itself. The Muscatatuck Regional Slope starts only a few miles west of the Richmond strip, falls to a lowland, the Scottsburg Lowland, then rises again to the Norman Upland. An unusual feature of this area is the Knobstone Escarpment strip, which is most prominent north of New Albany. Farther to the west, the land falls again to a plain strip, the Mitchell Plain, most notable for the world-famous Bedford limestone and the many sinkholes and caves formed in that limestone. It moves upward and westward again into a strip of greater relief, the Crawford Upland, then falls into the Wabash Lowland strip of moderate relief, and the meeting of the Wabash, White, and Ohio rivers.

Indiana is a unique and diverse place. Its rich history and culture are

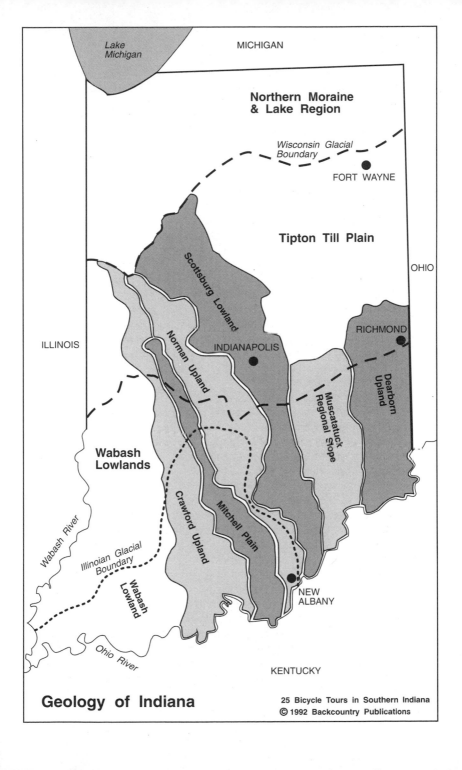

Geology of Indiana

25 Bicycle Tours in Southern Indiana
© 1992 Backcountry Publications

tied in with the opening of the frontier and the distinctive land the pioneers found here. Indians and fur traders were followed by settlers who brought diverse cultures and religions to the region. They followed the streams, trails, and buffalo traces and built their homes, canals, railroads, and roads to take their products to market. These are roads that cyclists can now use to tour Indiana.

The Tours

The highlights of the tours in this book are described in the first paragraph of each chapter. Choose a tour that suits your interests according to that description, then adjust the tour or your cycling to meet your particular needs. When selecting a tour, keep in mind the terrain, the ride's length, and the wind conditions.

In Indiana, when we say "hills," we usually mean short steep hills. They may only take a couple of minutes to climb, but you will probably need a 40-to-50-inch gear to climb them if you are a strong cyclist, a 30-to-40-inch gear if you are a moderate cyclist, and a 20-to-30-inch gear if you are on a fully loaded tandem. The hill in Brown County State Park (Tour 16) climbing up to the campsites is about as steep as most hills in Indiana, and the ones climbing out of the Ohio River valley are among the longest. One of my riding companions says, "I've never found a hill too steep to walk."

Many of the roads in Indiana are laid out in one-mile squares. A county road with a number, like 600N, means that the road lies six miles north of the county seat, running east and west. (Don't interpret the "N" to mean that the road runs north-south!) Thus, 650E would be a road 6.5 miles east of the county seat, running north and south. Keep this numbering system in mind when you cross county lines. A 600N road can suddenly become 800N because they are measured from two different county seats.

Not all of Indiana's roads are marked with a sign at the corner. This presented a problem when laying out the tours, and it will present a problem when taking the tours. If the road is not named then it is probably because there is no sign at the corner. In this case tourists are told something like, "left at the first opportunity." That means turn left at the next chance that isn't a driveway. Additionally, the tours all have a running mileage listed, so it is a good idea to know how far it is to the next turn and keep track of that on your cyclometer.

One thing you should consider when choosing a ride is that the supposedly easy rides are usually out in the open on flat land. This means that you need to be concerned about the wind. A 20-to-30-mph headwind out on the flats is actually much more difficult to handle than a few hills.

When you go on a tour, you might want to stay overnight in the city where the tour starts. It is also possible to stay in a town close by and drive or ride to the beginning of the tour. You could also stay somewhere along the route and start the tour in the middle.

Weekenders are two-day tours, designed to be enjoyed over an entire weekend. They give you an opportunity to enjoy a longer tour without riding all of it in one day. Ride to the midpoint, spend the night, then continue the tour the next day.

Cycling is much more fun when you're strong, so train and get strong. If there is a weaker rider in your group, choose a ride that is compatible with that rider's strength.

Tours can be shortened by:

- staying overnight at the midpoint of a one-day tour, thus making it a weekender;
- taking the shorter side of a loop twice;
- visiting an interesting city by bike, touring the city, but not taking the rest of the tour;
- motor vehicles can be useful in different ways:
  — leave one car at the end of the ride, and take another to the beginning of the ride;
  — have a driver drop you off somewhere and pick you up later at an agreed-upon place;
  — ask someone to follow your group in a sag vehicle, so that tired riders or those with mechanical difficulties can be transported.

Rides can be lengthened by:

- adding two rides together;
- doing a weekender in one day;
- taking side trips;
- being creative, and enjoying the routes according to your needs and cycling ability.

Safety

Cycle safely, be cautious, ride defensively, and follow the laws of Indiana. Don't assume that just because you, a cyclist, move more slowly than automobile traffic that automobile drivers are superior. They are not, but they can be dangerous, so be careful. Cycling safety is a matter of taking your space without taking too much, and deciding how much space is yours.

Indiana laws are reasonably simple for cyclists because they are mostly the same as for automobile drivers. Ride on the right. Stop at lights, signs, T intersections, and unsigned crossroads. Signal for turns and stops. Ride with lights and reflectors at night. One law specific to bicyclists is that they should ride as close to the right side of the road as practicable.

I have some additional suggestions based on eighteen years of cycling in Indiana. Don't ride at night, but if you must, be sure that you have lights and reflectors so that you can be seen. Between thirty and thirty-five people are killed in Indiana every year on bikes. About half of them are riding at night on country roads without a light. Tragically, most of them are children.

Wear a helmet. Should you get hit by a car, the odds that you will survive increase radically if you are wearing a helmet. Most cycling injuries, however, don't involve cars at all. Remember Walt Kelly's "Pogo"? He said, "We have met the enemy and he is us." Most cycling accidents involve a cyclist and perhaps a dog, a pothole, a railroad track, a slick road, or another cyclist.

If you fall from a bicycle without a helmet, you can be knocked unconscious. You will probably recover from that, but you may not. It will certainly be easier for your friends to take care of you if you are conscious. A final reason for wearing a helmet is that it marks you as a serious adult cyclist with motorists.

Ride to the right. The closest to the right that it is practicable to ride is about two feet from the edge of a road with no berm. (If there is a nice berm, then ride it.) It takes a better cyclist than I am to ride the right hand white line. There are too many potholes, dead animals, gravel, auto parts, and glass shards. Riding the white line also encourages some motorists to pass you when there isn't room. They perceive that there is no risk in doing so, because there is no risk to them. There is, however, considerable risk to you, and it is up to you to reduce your risk as best you can. Forcing them to face the real danger involved in passing you is not unreasonable. Don't expect all of them to appreciate their education, however.

Ride with friends. It is always a good idea to ride with friends, both for enjoyment and for safety. People get sick, they have flats, they get tired, they overheat-lots of reasons to have a friend along.

Indiana is no more dangerous than any of the other states I have cycled in, and it is less dangerous than many. In Indiana most motorists will treat you with respect, give you a microwave, and go on about their business. I hope you wave back and give them the respect to which they are entitled. Most of all, I hope that you adore cycling through Indiana as much as I do. For more information on cycling, read Norman D. Ford's book, *Keep on Pedaling: The Complete Guide to Adult Bicycling* (The Countryman Press, Woodstock, Vermont). See you on the road!

Chuck Fearnow

Sources of Tour Planning Information for Indiana
Department of Natural Resources Maps:

The following maps are available from the Indiana Department of Natural Resources. It is advisable to first send for their catalog, which lists the other maps (USGS and Hoosier Bikeway System) and shows their relative locations. The catalog is free.

- U.S. Geological Survey Maps. The series 1-degree-by-2-degree Topographic Quadrangle maps, scale 1:250,000 (approx. 1/4 inch per mile) are available for $4.20 each, plus $3.00 shipping via UPS. These maps show elevation contour lines, as well as churches, schools, and other landmarks.
- U.S. Geological Survey Maps. The series 1:100,000 map is 1/4 of the 1-degree-by-2-degree map. It, too, shows elevation contour lines, as well as churches, schools, and other landmarks. It covers less area, but it contains much more detail. It is the same price as the 1-degree-by-2-degree map.
- Hoosier Bikeway System. A series of bicycle tours has been developed, and guidebooks are now available for eleven tours. Each guidebook contains detailed maps, instructions, and associated information for navigating the tours. The base maps are USGS topographic maps at a scale of 15/16 inches equals one mile. The tours are marked on primarily lightly traveled roads, through quiet towns and scenic countryside, connecting state recreation areas. Each guidebook contains several strip maps, accompanied by elevation cross-sections and information on tour markings. Each is made to use in a handlebar bag map pouch. The tours are also marked on the pavement. Guidebooks are $1.00 each.
- Indianapolis Bicycle Users Map. This is a detailed street map of Indianapolis and Marion County, with streets coded as to suitability for bicycle travel. It is available at most Indianapolis bicycle stores or by mail and costs $2.00.

The above maps are available from Department of Natural Resources,Map Sales Unit,402 West Washington Street, W160,Indianapolis, IN 46204,or call (317) 232-4180. Make your check payable to Indiana Department of Natural Resources.

Department of Transportation Map (The Indiana Official Highway Map.) This map shows all numbered federal and state roads, along with an index of towns. It also identifies the county seat towns. The map is free and can be obtained from Indiana Department of Transportation, Public Information, Room 1101, State Office Building, Indianapolis, IN 46204, or call (317) 232-5115.

Rising Sun Courthouse

County Maps

Two companies in Indianapolis furnish county maps prepared by the State of Indiana. These maps show the numbers of U.S. and state highways only. They do *not* show county road names or numbers. The state does not furnish these maps directly to users. The maps are at 1/2-inch-to-the-mile scale and 1-inch-to-the-mile scale. They can be purchased from Marbaugh Engineering and Supply, 121 West North Street, Indianapolis, IN 46205, or call (317) 632-4322 or from Odyssey Map Store, 148 North Delaware Street, Indianapolis, IN 46204, or call (317) 635-3837.

Indiana County Maps, a 128-page, 11-by-16-inch book, contains 1/2-inch-to-the-mile maps of all ninety-two Indiana counties; an index to the counties and towns; and a short history of each county. It is available by sending $14.85 to County Maps, Puetz Place, Lyndon Station, WI 53944, or call (608) 666-3331.This book of maps can also be purchased in or ordered from a map store in your local community.

State Parks

Recreation Guide is a booklet detailing the facilities available in Indiana State Parks. It is free from Division of State Parks, 402 West Washington Street, Room 298, Indianapolis, IN 46204 or call 1-800-622-4931, or (317) 232-4124 in Indianapolis.

The Indiana Department of Commerce, Tourism Development Division, publishes the following guides:

- *Indiana Camping guide.* This large foldout lists public and commercial campgrounds and recreation areas in Indiana by region.
- *Indiana Festivals Guide.* These brochures are available for spring/summer and winter/fall. They list dozens of community events which can be both entertaining and interesting.
- *Indiana Attractions.* This 120-page book lists the amusements, arts, historic sites, and museums in Indiana cities alphabetically. It also lists visitor and convention bureaus and state parks.

These sources are available from Department of Commerce, Tourism Development Division, One North Capital, Indianapolis, IN 46204 or call 1 800-289-6646, or (317) 232-8860 in Indianapolis.

There are two national sources for maps and information that you might also be interested in. *Bikecentennial* has wonderful cross-country maps if you are interested in an extended tour. These and other Bikecentennial maps can be used locally and regionally as well. It can be ordered from Bikecentennial, P.O. Box 8308, Missoula, MT 59807, or call (406) 721-1776

League of American Wheelmen (L.A.W.) has touring information directors in each of the states who are available for local information. They also publish *Bicycle USA* and an almanac that gives terrific information about maps, books, information contacts, clubs, and events in every state. These can be ordered from League of American Wheelmen (L.A.W.), 90 West Ostend Street, Suite 120, Baltimore, MD 21230

Before you send any money or order any materials, we strongly suggest that you call and confirm the address and price, since they occasionally change.

1

Utopia

35 miles; moderately easy

The main feature of this tour is New Harmony, a restored settlement that was founded in 1814, two years before Indiana became a state. Give yourself plenty of time for this one and bring your walking shoes. Other sights on this route include many oil wells, including a few in Harmonie State Park. Deer are numerous in the park, especially along the Wabash River in the morning and evening. Despite its fine facilities, the park is seldom as crowded as other parks in Indiana.

New Harmony was the site of two nineteenth-century communal living experiments. The first was that of the Rappites, a religious sect. Immediately following them came a group led by Robert Owen, an industrialist and philanthropist. Although Owen's community failed after only two years, he brought many intellectuals to the area who had a lasting impact.

Despite the town's small size, it takes about five hours to see all the sights. On weekends during the summer, you may be able to see a play or concert at Thrall's Opera House or Murphy Auditorium. New Harmony also has a very fine restaurant, the Red Geranium. If you would rather stay in a hotel than camp at the park, try the New Harmony Inn.

0.0 **START at Harmonie State Park onto IN 269.**

0.9 **RIGHT onto IN 69.**

5.8 **LEFT at the fourth opportunity.**
You should see a sign that says "To Springfield 2 Miles."

8.1 **CONTINUE through the small town of Springfield (which has no facilities).**

14.7 **LEFT at the T-stay on the paved road.**

15.9 **CROSS IN 66 in Wadesville.**

15.9 **LEFT at the stop sign.**
There is a restaurant and a minimart in town.

16.2 **RIGHT at the T onto IN 66.**

16.5   RIGHT onto IN 165.

20.5   CONTINUE onto IN 165 as it turns east to go into Poseyville.

At the H&R Pharmacy in town, there is an old-fashioned soda fountain that serves shakes, malts, phosphates, and freshly squeezed lemonade. There is also a restaurant in town. Notice the two beautiful old bank buildings. One of them is now used as a church.

21.1   RIGHT onto Cale Street in Poseyville.

21.2 Notice the Carnegie Public Library on the right.

21.4   RIGHT onto Pine Street.

21.8   LEFT at the T onto Lockwood Avenue.

21.9   LEFT onto IN 68.

You are leaving Poseyville.

29.4   RIGHT at the T onto IN 66.

You are entering New Harmony.

There are too many sights in town to list them all here. This route will take you to the Athenaeum, where you can buy your tour tickets

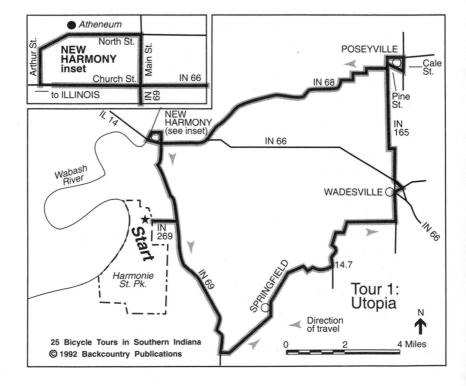

and get a map. Just follow the signs to the Athenaeum.

New Harmony was founded by a religious group known as the Harmonists, or Rappites, in honor of their founder, George Rapp. Rapp was born in the German province of Würtemberg in 1757. He separated from the state-controlled Lutheran Church in 1785 to become the leader of a group of dissenters who met illegally in his home. In 1791, as the number of his followers increased, the civilian authorities became alarmed and attempted to silence him. Rapp refused to submit, and after a brief imprisonment his popularity increased and his following grew to twenty thousand. The Würtemberg government demanded that he submit a written statement of his faith in 1798. Rapp complied, and the statement showed the Rappites were opposed to infant baptism and military service. They acknowledged the authority of civilian government, but they believed people had the right to form separate congregations and schools to promote their own beliefs. Local authorities regarded this as open rebellion, so in 1803 Rapp decided to seek haven in America.

George Rapp attempted unsuccessfully to purchase land in Ohio and Indiana. Many of his followers began migrating to the United States and their early arrival forced him to settle for a site north of Pittsburgh. In 1805, approximately five hundred charter members signed the Articles of Association that formed the Harmony Society in Harmony, Pennsylvania. The members turned over all their property to the Society and agreed to abide by its rules and promote its interests. The Society pledged to all its members complete access to its religious and educational benefits and all the necessities of life. In 1807 and 1808 they experienced a religious revival and renounced sexual relations.

The Harmonites purchased the land for New Harmony in 1814. They bought enough territory to secure exclusive control of the Wabash River for several miles and to provide a buffer against their neighbors. Although many died of malaria during their first year here, the community later became very prosperous. They fenced and cultivated two to three thousand acres. Their fields and orchards contained a wide variety of crops and animals. In 1819 the Harmonists produced $12,000 worth of agricultural produce, and in 1820 they sold $50,000 worth of manufactured goods. Orders from Harmonist members were filled for free, but outsiders often complained about the high prices they were charged.

In 1824, George Rapp sold New Harmony to Robert Owen for $150,000 and moved his followers back to Pennsylvania, where he formed a new town named Economy, located just a few miles down the Ohio River from Pittsburgh. After this move, the Harmony Society began to decline. The beautiful young Hildegard Mutschler,

The Roofless Church in New Harmony

Rapp's companion and laboratory assistant, ran away with another Harmonist member in 1829. After Rapp condemned his remaining followers for causing her departure, some members left the Society. About one-third of the remaining members left in 1832 to follow Bernhard Mueller, who claimed to possess the philosopher's stone, which could produce gold.

The Harmonists had always believed that Christ was about to return to Earth and that they were the chosen people. This is why they believed in celibacy, although the policy was not strictly enforced. George Rapp died in 1847, but the Harmony Society lasted until 1916. The movement lost strength as the predicted end of the world and the return of Christ did not materialize.

For more information on the Rappites, read "New Harmony's First Utopians," by Donald E. Pitzer and Josephine M. Elliot, in *Indiana Magazine of History*, Vol. 75 (September 1979).

31.0   CONTINUE straight on Church Street when IN 66 and 69 intersect.

31.2   RIGHT onto Arthur Street.
(If you miss this turn, you will wind up in Illinois, which is not on the tour.)

31.3   PARK at the Athenaeum, get your tickets, and see the town.
While you're there you may want to make reservations at the Red

Geranium or get play tickets (at Thrall's Opera House or Murphy Auditorium) for the evening.

31.3   HEAD east on North Street.

31.6   RIGHT on Main Street.

32.2   On your right is a re-creation of the Rappites' Labyrinth, built close to its original site. This maze-shaped hedge was created to symbolize the tortuous path to heaven. Visitors are welcome to walk through the maze, but please do not take shortcuts to the center, since this damages the hedge. Besides, no one ever made it to heaven by cheating!

34.6   RIGHT onto IN 269.

35.5   ENTER Harmonie State Park.

Camping
Harmonie State Park, Route 1, Box 5A, New Harmony IN 47631, (812) 682-4821.

Hotel
The New Harmony Inn, P.O. Box 581, New Harmony IN 47631, (812) 682-4491.
New Harmony Tours: Historic New Harmony, P.O. Box 579, New Harmony IN 47631, (812) 682-4482.

Bicycle Repair Services
Dan's Bicycle Center, 213 North Main, Mt. Vernon, IN 47620 (812) 838-2691.

2

Evansville

25 miles; easy riding, but heavy traffic

This tour covers the old riverside district of Evansville, featuring tree-lined streets and old river homes. The Ohio River was one of the main sources of travel and commerce in the Midwest's early settlement. The tour passes the remnants of an Indian town that flourished more than five hundred years ago.

The tour starts at Riverfront Park. Enter the park from the intersection of Riverside and Court streets.

0.0 START at Riverfront Park.
Turn right as you exit the park.

0.1 LEFT on Cherry Street.

0.2 RIGHT on First Street.
This is the heart of the Riverside Historic District. There are many fine old homes along the tree-lined streets. Unfortunately, the brick

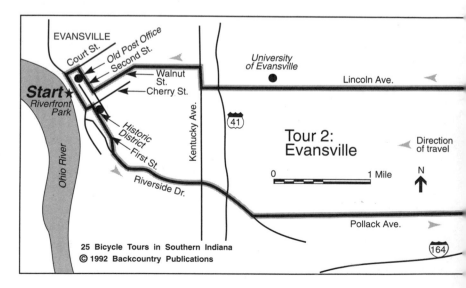

25 Bicycle Tours in Southern Indiana
© 1992 Backcountry Publications

streets are not very comfortable for bike riding.

The John Augustus Reitz home is the only such home open to the public. It is slightly off the route (at 224 Southeast First Street). Reitz built the home in 1871 after making his fortune in the lumber business.

For more information, contact the Reitz Home Museum, 224 Southeast First Street, Evansville,IN 47713 (812) 426-1871.

0.9   LEFT at the T on Riverside Drive.

2.7   LEFT on Pollack Avenue.

7.5   Angel Mounds State Historic Site was an Indian town of about a thousand inhabitants between A.D. 1300 and 1500.

A portion of the stockade wall has been reconstructed. The wall surrounded the town, except for the side that bordered the Ohio River. Several Indian homes have also been rebuilt. Several Indian mounds are on this site, the largest of which is forty-four feet high and covers four acres. No one knows why the Indians abandoned this site.

For more information, contact Angel Mounds State Historic Site, 8215 Pollack Avenue, Evansville, IN 47715 (812) 853-3956.

9.0   RIGHT at the T onto IN 662.

Be careful-this section of the route has the heaviest traffic, especially as you enter the town of Newburgh. Newburgh was the scene of the first Confederate raid into Indiana during the Civil War. Newburgh Road's name changes to Jennings Street in town, then to French Island.

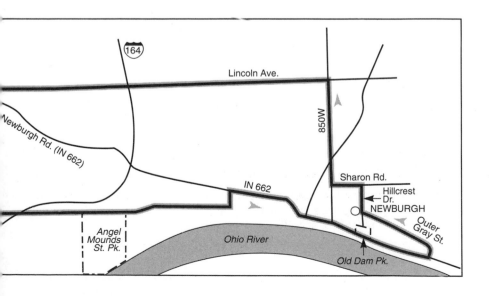

Reconstructed Indian dwellings at Angel Mounds

    10.7 Old Dam Park is on the right along the Ohio River. Upstream is a set of locks on the river.

11.6   **LEFT on Outer Gray Street.**

12.8   **RIGHT at the T onto Hillcrest Drive.**

13.1   **LEFT at the T onto Sharon Road.**

13.4   **RIGHT at the T.**

13.7   **CONTINUE straight onto 850W, as the main road bends to the right.**

14.6   **LEFT at the intersection onto Lincoln Avenue (which is unmarked).**
        (To find several fast-food restaurants, continue straight instead for about a half-mile.)

19.0   **RIGHT at the T onto Newburgh Road. This road becomes Lincoln Avenue.**

21.6   To the right is the University of Evansville, a private school with more than six thousand students.

22.4   RIGHT on Kentucky Avenue.

22.7   LEFT on Walnut Street. Stay with Walnut Street as it bears left.

24.1   RIGHT on Second Street.

24.4   The Old U.S. Post Office, on the left, was built in 1879. It has since been refurbished and is now used for other purposes.

24.4   LEFT on Court Street.

24.6   ENTER Riverfront Park.

Bicycle Repair Services

Bicycle World, 3810 East Morgan Avenue, Evansville, IN 47715 (812) 473-2453.

Gilles Schwinn Cycle, 2346 Washington Avenue, Evansville, IN 47714 (812) 422-6800.

Gilles Schwinn Cyclery, 200-D South Greenriver Road, Evansville, IN 47715 (812) 477-8828

Gilles Schwinn Cyclery, 2901 1st Avenue, Evansville, IN 47710 (812) 422-6800.

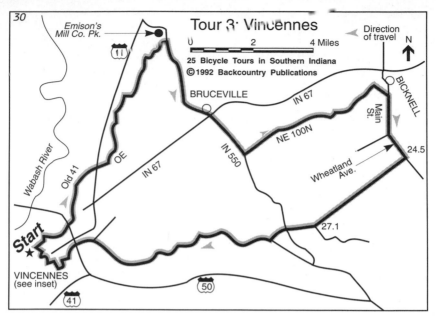

Tour 3: Vincennes

0   2   4 Miles

25 Bicycle Tours in Southern Indiana
©1992 Backcountry Publications

Direction of travel

N

Emison's Mill Co. Pk.

11

BRUCEVILLE

IN 67

BICKNELL

Main St.

NE 100N

24.5

IN 550

Wheatland Ave.

Wabash River

OE

Old 41

IN 67

27.1

Start

VINCENNES
(see inset)

50

41

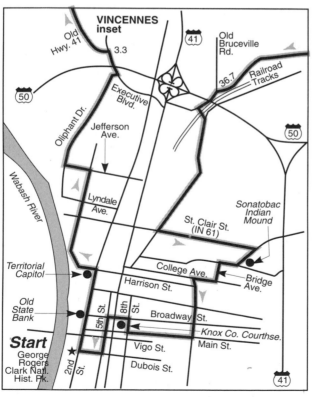

VINCENNES inset

Old Hwy. 41

3.3

41

Old Bruceville Rd.

36.7

Railroad Tracks

50

Executive Blvd.

Oliphant Dr.

Jefferson Ave.

Lyndale Ave.

50

Wabash River

St. Clair St. (IN 61)

Sonatobac Indian Mound

College Ave.

Bridge Ave.

Territorial Capitol

Harrison St.

Old State Bank

Broadway St.

8th St.

5th St.

Knox Co. Courthse.

Main St.

Start
George Rogers Clark Natl. Hist. Pk.

2nd St.

Vigo St.

Dubois St.

41

3

Vincennes

42 miles; moderate, with a few easy hills

French trappers, Indians, presidents, forts, and a comedian are the highlights of this Knox County trip. Vincennes was the capital of the Indiana Territory. It was also the scene of many battles for control with the British during the American Revolution. William Henry Harrison, territorial governor and later president, lived here; George Rogers Clark fought here; and comodian Red Skelton lived here too.

French trappers were the first white men to move into this area. Sieur de Vincennes was ordered to build a chain of forts to halt British expansion in the New World. He built the fort at Vincennes in 1732. After he was taken prisoner by the Chickasaw Indians and burned at the stake in 1736, the fort was named Post St. Vincennes.

The British drove the French out of North America in 1763 and took control of the fort, which they renamed Fort Sackville. During the American Revolution, George Rogers Clark, a young Virginian, led a small group of volunteers who captured Fort Sackville in the summer of 1778. He went on to capture Cahokia and Kaskaskia, two forts in Illinois. Colonel Hamilton of the British— also known as "Hair-Buyer Hamilton" because he bought American scalps from the Indians—moved south from Detroit and retook Vincennes in November 1778.

After hearing that the British had once again occupied Fort Sackville, Clark took immediate action. In the middle of winter, while the Illinois Territory was flooded, he decided to march on Vincennes, hoping to take Colonel Hamilton by surprise. Clark, who had only 175 men instead of the five hundred he had originally hoped for, wrote to his governor, Patrick Henry, "Great things have been effected by a few men well conducted." His plan worked to perfection. The Americans surrounded the fort, created the illusion that their force was much larger than it actually was, and convinced the British to surrender. With this brilliant stroke, Americans assumed control of the Midwest.

Start the trip by visiting the George Rogers Clark National Historic Park. There are several interesting displays here, and a short but informative film about Clark's military exploits. The George Rogers Clark Memorial has seven murals that depict scenes from his campaign during the Revolution. In the center is a statue of Clark.

0.0   START at the George Rogers Clark National Historic Park.
        (The parking lot closes at 5:00 P.M., so park on the side street if you
        won't be back before then.)

0.0   LEFT (northeast) on Second Street.
        Cross Vigo Street, which was named for Francis Vigo, a wealthy fur
        trader who financially supported George Rogers Clark's military
        campaigns. To the west this street crosses the Wabash River. It
        follows the path of the Buffalo Trace, an ancient migratory route
        taken by the buffalo. It was later used by Indians and early pioneers,
        including one named Abraham Lincoln when his family moved from
        Indiana to Illinois. The bridge has a sculpture of a young Abe on the
        Illinois side and is named the Lincoln Memorial Bridge.

0.2   RIGHT to stay on Second Street.

        0.3   On the left is the Old State Bank, chartered in 1834. It is the
        oldest surviving bank building in Indiana. The second floor of the
        building was used for board meetings, and the two clerks slept on
        the third floor to make sure it wasn't robbed. Only the first floor was
        open to the public. Fur traders and other "men of odor" were
        permitted only in the back section, and they had to use a side
        entrance. The bank vault was imported from France. The building's
        original lead roof was removed during the Civil War and used to
        make bullets.

0.8   LEFT on Harrison Street.

        0.9   To the left is the territorial capitol. This is a small two-story
        building, and a replica of the Western Sun print shop. The Western
        Sun was Indiana's first newspaper. A little farther south and west is
        Grouseland, the home of William Henry Harrison, Indiana's first
        territorial governor. This fine mansion was built in 1804 and was
        named for the abundant grouse in the area, which Harrison liked to
        hunt. The Shawnee Chief Tecumseh and Harrison once met on the
        lawn. They were, however, unable to resolve their differences, and
        in 1811 Harrison marched northward to defeat The Prophet,
        Tecumseh's brother, in the Battle of Tippecanoe.

1.0   LEFT at the stop sign. Cross Lyndale Avenue.
        Richard Bernard Skelton, better known as Red, was born on this
        street in 1913. When he was twelve, he left town to join a traveling
        medicine show. Red had his own TV show for many years and is
        best known for his characters Freddy the Freeloader and Clem
        Kadiddlehopper.

1.8   LEFT on Jefferson Avenue.

2.1   RIGHT on Oliphant Drive.

2.3   **CONTINUE straight, crossing a small stream.**

3.0   **LEFT at the T on Executive Boulevard.**

3.3   **LEFT on Old Highway 41N.**

5.4   **RIGHT at second opportunity, and cross US 41.**
The road is now called "OE."

10.8   **RIGHT at the T onto IN 550.**
Just to your left on IN 550 is Emisons Mill County Park (which has pit toilets, a water fountain, and picnic shelters). Near this spot, Harrison's men camped on their way to the Battle of Tippecanoe. According to legend, the militiamen from Kentucky admired the Blue Grass in the meadow so much, they took seed back home with them. Today, Kentucky is known as the Bluegrass State.

13.6   **ENTER the town of Bruceville.**
There are soda machines and minimarts along IN 67. The town is named after William Bruce, Abraham Lincoln once stayed at Bruce's home while campaigning for Whig presidential candidate Henry Clay.

15.9   **LEFT on NE 100N.**

21.0   **RIGHT on Third Street in Bicknell.**
There are several restaurants in town. In the early 1900s this was a major coal-mining center. Since the 1940s, the coal business in this area has declined significantly.

21.0   **LEFT on Vigo Street.**

21.3   **RIGHT on Seventh Street.**

21.4   **BEAR RIGHT (don't make the acute right) onto Main Street.**

22.0   **LEFT on Wheatland Avenue.**

24.5   **STAY on main road as it curves to the right.**

27.1   **CONTINUE STRAIGHT when the main road curves left. The road for the next few miles is a little rough.**

29.3   **CROSS IN 550.**

30.0   **RIGHT at the T.**

36.7   **LEFT onto Old Bruceville Road in Vincennes.**

37.0   **LEFT at the first opportunity.**

37.0   **CROSS the railroad tracks.**

37.1   **RIGHT at the T.**

Francis Vigo

38.2   LEFT on IN 61, or St. Clair Street.

39.1   ACUTE RIGHT at the T.

> 39.2   Sonatobac Indian Mound is on the left. It was built about 300 B.C. for ceremonial purposes. The site was deserted in about A.D. 2 after a flood. It was named for the son of Tabac, a local Piankashaw Indian chief who offered to help George Rogers Clark during his campaign to take Fort Sackville.

39.5   LEFT on Bridge Avenue.

39.7   RIGHT at the T onto College Avenue.

39.9   LEFT at the first opportunity.

40.4   RIGHT on Main Street.

41.0   RIGHT on Eighth Street.

> 41.1   The Knox County Courthouse was built in 1876.

41.1   LEFT on Broadway Street.

> 41.2   On the northeast corner of the courthouse square is a Civil War monument.

41.3   LEFT on Fifth Street.

41.6   RIGHT on Dubois Street.

41.8   RETURN to George Rogers Clark Memorial.
> Food is available at the Market Street Station, in downtown Vincennes on First Street, and at Marone's Formosa Gardens, on Second.

Bicycle Repair Services
Schaeffer's Schwinn, 1717 Hart, Vincennes, IN 47591 (812) 882-5588.
Weston's Bike Shop, 2038 Washington Avenue, Vincennes, IN 47591 (812-882-6455).

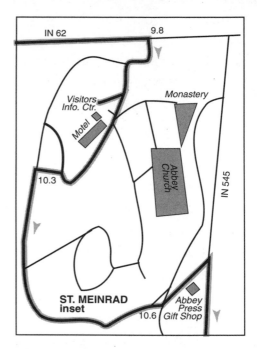

IN 62   9.8

Visitors Info. Ctr.   *Monastery*

Motel

10.3

Abbey Church

IN 545

Abbey Press Gift Shop

10.6

ST. MEINRAD
inset

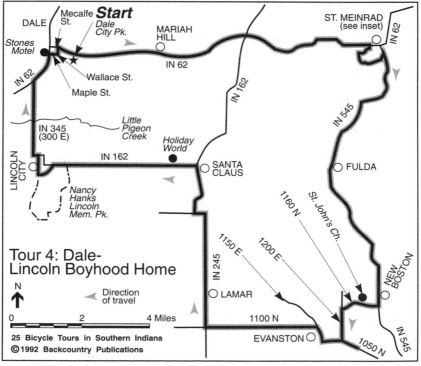

Mecalfe St.   **Start**

DALE   *Dale City Pk.*   MARIAH HILL   ST. MEINRAD (see inset)   IN 62

Stones Motel

Wallace St.

IN 62   IN 62

Maple St.

IN 162

IN 545

IN 345 (300 E)   *Little Pigeon Creek*   *Holiday World*

LINCOLN CITY   IN 162   SANTA CLAUS   FULDA

Nancy Hanks Lincoln Mem. Pk.

1160 N   St. John's Ch.

Tour 4: Dale-Lincoln Boyhood Home

N

1150 E   1200 E   NEW BOSTON

IN 245   LAMAR   IN 545

Direction of travel

0   2   4 Miles

1100 N   EVANSTON   1050 N

25 Bicycle Tours in Southern Indiana
©1992 Backcountry Publications

4

Dale-Lincoln Boyhood Home

40 miles; moderately hilly

Saint Meinrad, Santa Claus, and Abraham Lincoln's boyhood home are along this Spencer County route. Saint Meinrad is an archabbey and seminary that trains priests. The grounds are beautiful, as are the church and abbey. The stained glass windows in the church are worth the trip. The Santa Claus Post Office is quite busy every Christmas, when thousands of people send mail that they want postmarked from Santa Claus. Also in Santa Claus is Holiday World, a large amusement park. The Lincoln boyhood home is a brief tour and a good bike break before returning to Dale. This simple working farm recreates the farm where Lincoln lived when he was a boy in Indiana. Few places offer the flavor of Indiana living in the early 1800s that this farm does.

The tour begins in Dale, which lies just south of Interstate 64 on IN 231. As you come into town on IN 231, IN 62 intersects IN 231. Turn right on IN 62 for two blocks to the city park. You will pass Windells Restaurant, a good place to get breakfast. Also in Dale is the Stones Motel, if you would like to stay overnight; there are also a couple of other places to stay on the interstate. Along the route is the Saint Meinrad motel, located on the grounds of the archabbey. Accommodations there are simple, but if you stay there, you can spend time touring the abbey at the beginning or end of the ride. About twenty miles south of Dale, on IN 231, is Rockport, where there is a bed and breakfast in a home that was built circa 1857. It is a wonderful place to stay. In the evening it's the local hot spot for dinner.

Also along the route is the Nancy Hanks Lincoln Memorial State Park, which offers excellent accommodations for campers.

0.0   **START at the Dale City Park on IN 62, at the intersection of Medcalfe and Wallace streets.**

0.0   **RIGHT (East) on 62.**

3.2   **ENTER Mariah Hill (where there is a restaurant).**

5.9   **CROSS IN 162 at the four-way stop.**

9.2   **ENTER the town of St. Meinrad.**

9.8   RIGHT at the archabbey sign.

9.9   ENTER the St. Meinrad Archabbey and Seminary.

10.0   LEFT at the Y toward the visitors information center and the motel office.

St. Meinrad Archabbey offers three types of tours; a self-guided tour on paper, a self-guided tour with an audiocassette, and a personally guided tour. The Romanesque abbey church is made of St. Meinrad sandstone. It was completed in 1907 by the Benedictine monks and the people of St. Meinrad. In 1969 the church underwent extensive remodeling to adapt to the new liturgy and to restore the church to the simplicity of the Romanesque design.

The beautiful windows in the church were painted in 1908 by the Royal Bavarian Art Institute of F. X. Zettler of Munich, Germany. The organ was installed in the 1950s and has since undergone extensive renovation. The image of Christ in the apse of the church was painted by Father Gregory deWit, a monk of Mont Cesar Abbey in Belgium. Father Gregory also did the paintings of Saint Benedict and Saint Meinrad in the memorial lobby of Sherwood Hall.

10.1   RIGHT out of the visitors information center parking lot at the visitors information sign.

10.2   BEAR RIGHT through the additional parking lot behind the motel.

10.2   LEFT at the Y, at the end of the parking lot. Ride downhill slowly.

10.3   LEFT at the T, with the Stop sign. Follow the road as it curves around the grounds.

10.6   RIGHT at the Y. You are still on the archabbey grounds.

10.8   RIGHT into the Abbey Press gift shop.

Yes, this is the Abbey Press of mail-order fame. The shop offers all the items displayed in the catalog, plus other religious articles.

10.8   RIGHT out of the gift shop parking lot.

10.9   RIGHT (South) onto IN 545.

14.6   ENTER Fulda where there is a food mart and restaurant.

19.0   ENTER New Boston.

19.4   RIGHT at the St. John's Lutheran Church sign.

This road is unmarked, but it is 1160N. It is the first road after the New Boston town limits sign. Pass the church about a half-mile down the road.

20.5   LEFT at the T, on 1200E.

21.6 RIGHT at the T, on 1050N.

22.2 RIGHT at the Y, on 1150E. Enter Evanston.

22.8 LEFT at the Y, on 1100N.
Indiana has a few oil wells in the southern part of the state. There was a time when a great deal of natural gas was taken from the state.

26.2 RIGHT at the T on IN 245.

27.4 ENTER Lamar.

30.0 RIGHT at the Y, to stay on IN 245.

30.5 ENTER Santa Claus.

31.8 The Santa Claus Post Office does a "land office" business at Christmastime. People from all over the country mail their Christmas cards to Santa Claus so that they will bear the Santa Claus postmark.

32.1 The Holiday World Amusement Park was America's first theme park. It originated in the 1940s and is open from May through October. The three theme sections are Halloween, the Fourth of July, and Santa Claus Land. In the summer of 1989 Holiday World added outdoor air conditioning to its Halloween section. Tiny droplets of water are sprayed into the air to cool it by as much as twenty degrees. The park features fifty rides, shows, and attractions, including Frightful Falls, live shows, scale-model riverboats, Bavarian glass-blowers, more than fifty wax figures of famous Americans, a collection of two thousand dolls, lots of food, and other attractions.

32.1 CONTINUE on IN 162 (West).
Pass Christmas Lake, which has groceries and a drugstore.

36.5 Nancy Hanks Lincoln Memorial State Park is on the left.

36.5 RIGHT at the Lincoln National Boyhood Memorial.

36.6 RIGHT at the memorial's visitors center.
Continue straight here if you don't wish to go to the visitors center.

36.7 RIGHT out of the visitors center.

37.1 RIGHT at the Living History Farm.
Try to imagine how Abraham Lincoln grew up. It's hard, but it becomes much easier at the Living History Farm. The National Park Service preserves and operates this authentic working pioneer farm on the site of the original Lincoln homestead. Abe moved here in 1816 when he was seven and Indiana had just become a state. Here he split logs for the rail fence that kept the wild animals out of

St. Meinrad Archabbey

the fields; plowed, planted, and harvested food with his family; and here that he read by candlelight. Here his mother and sister died, and here he grew into a man.

37.2   RIGHT out of the Living History Farm.

37.4   LEFT at the T. Enter Lincoln City.

37.6   CONTINUE on IN 345 (also known as 300E).

38.8   CROSS Little Pigeon Creek.

39.9   RIGHT at the T, on IN 62, heading back toward Dale.

40.1   CONTINUE into Dale.

40.5 The Stones Motel is on the left. (It has a restaurant.)

40.7   RIGHT on Maple Street. Cross Main Street at the four-way stop.

40.8   LEFT on Wallace Street. Cross Vine and Locust streets.

41.0   RIGHT into Dale City Park and return to your car.

5

Orange County Loop

17 miles; difficult

If you have the impression that Indiana is nothing but flat farmland, cornfields and all, this tour will alter that impression greatly. Though it may be short in its mileage, it is a difficult ride with wonderful scenery and interesting towns to visit. This very hilly loop will rival any tough terrain you have ever tried. Be very careful to follow the directions and map, as the roads are not marked at all in the country. If you are going on this tour on a hot day, take plenty of water since there are not many towns along the way.

The tour starts at the town square in Paoli. There is ample parking around the square.

Paoli, the county seat of Orange County, was founded in 1816 and settled predominantly by Quakers from North Carolina. It was named after Pasquale Paoli Ashe, son of North Carolina governor Samuel Ashe.

The county courthouse was finished in 1850 and is made of stone and concrete, with several interesting iron staircases on its exterior. On the south side of the square is the Landmark Hotel. Formerly called the Mineral Springs Hotel, the hotel was marketed as a health resort, whose local mineral water was said to have great curative powers.

0.0   **Ride south on IN 37 from the town square.**
You are not going very far so consult the next line.

0.2   **RIGHT on Cherry Street.**
Cherry Street is marked not by a sign with its name but by a sign for the junior and senior high schools.

0.6   **LEFT on Elm Street.**
Elm Street curves through the junior-senior high school complex, heads into the country, and becomes Willow Creek Road.

2.2   **RIGHT on unmarked 150S at the T.**

2.7   **LEFT on unmarked 225W, at the T.**
225W curves to the west and becomes 325W.

4.7   **RIGHT at the Y, onto unmarked 325S.**

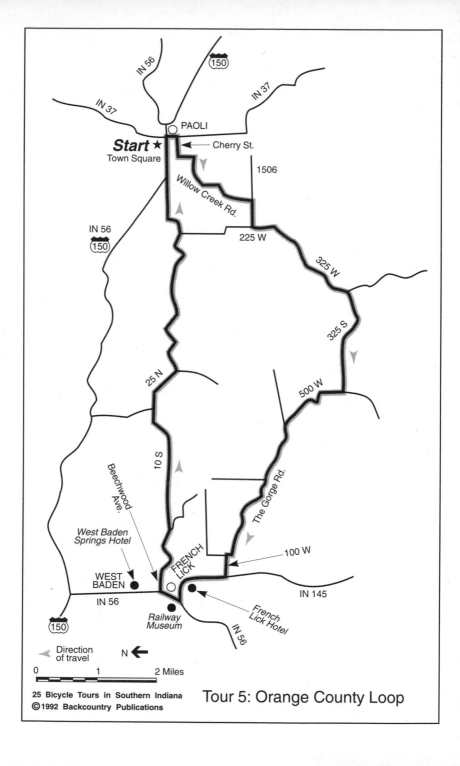

Start ★
Town Square

PAOLI

IN 56

150

IN 37

IN 37

Cherry St.

1506

Willow Creek Rd.

IN 56
150

225 W

325 W

325 S

25 N

500 W

10 S

The Gorge Rd.

Beechwood Ave.

West Baden Springs Hotel

FRENCH LICK

100 W

IN 145

WEST BADEN

French Lick Hotel

IN 56

150

Railway Museum

IN 56

Direction of travel

N

0   1   2 Miles

25 Bicycle Tours in Southern Indiana
©1992 Backcountry Publications

Tour 5: Orange County Loop

This intersection is marked by a sign for the Spring Valley National Forest and Campground. There is also a bait shop in a trailer at the intersection.

6.4   RIGHT on unmarked 500W, at the T.

7.6   LEFT at the Y, on unmarked The Gorge Road.

8.5   LEFT at the Y, staying on unmarked The Gorge Road.

8.9   LEFT at the Y by the Gentle Care of French Lick Nursing Home.
This unmarked road is 100S.

10.1   RIGHT on IN 145 and enter French Lick.
French Lick, along with its sister city West Baden, was once a thriving city known for its health resort, now called the French Lick Springs Hotel and Golf Resort, located on IN 56 in French Lick. French Lick's modern notoriety is for being the hometown of one of professional basketball's most dominant players, Larry Bird.

William A. Bowles built the French Lick Hotel in 1840 in order to capitalize on the high mineral and salt content of the local springs. I he hotel prospered throughout the nineteenth century as a health spa. After Bowles died in 1873, the hotel changed hands several times, and was badly damaged by fire in 1897. In 1901 the property came into the possession of a group of investors led by Thomas Taggert, who had been mayor of Indianapolis, chairman of the Democratic National Committee, and a U.S. Senator. The hotel was rebuilt, expanded, and gained international fame. Since 1946, the hotel has changed hands many times and is still a successful operation.

At the intersection of IN 145 and IN 56 is the Indiana Railway Museum. The museum, founded in 1961, had several homes in other cities before settling in French Lick in 1978. The museum offers an eighteen-mile ride on a steam train that takes you through the 2,217-foot Barton Tunnel. The museum also operates an electric trolley between the West Baden Springs Hotel and the French Lick Springs Hotel and Golf Resort.

11.0   RIGHT on IN 56, and enter West Baden.
West Baden is internationally known for the West Baden Springs Hotel. Called the Eighth Wonder of the World, it is the world's third-largest unsupported dome, surpassed only by the domed stadiums in New Orleans and Houston. Located at the north end of town on IN 56, the hotel came into existence in 1852. Several additions were made to include an opera house, casino, a bicycle racing track, and a pony track.

The hotel burned in 1901 and was reconstructed on an even grander scale in 1903 by architect Harrison Albright. Famous people and gangsters flocked to the hotel to enjoy gambling and stage shows, to ride horses and bicycles, and to play golf. The hotel closed in 1931 due to the Depression and was given to the Jesuits in 1934. The Jesuits stripped the hotel of its finery and converted it to a seminary. The Jesuits left in 1964, and it became a college, the Northwood Institute, in 1966. The college closed in 1983, and the structure is presently undergoing a massive renovation to convert it to its former glory.

11.3   RIGHT on Beechwood Avenue.

12.3   LEFT at the Y, onto unmarked 10S.

14.2   RIGHT at the Y, onto unmarked 25N.
This intersection is right in the middle of a steep grade.

15.1   LEFT at the Y, staying on unmarked 25N.
Follow this road through the country back to Paoli. You pass the Paoli Peaks Ski Resort at about 2 miles past the Y.

16.8   RIGHT on US 150/IN 56/IN 37.
Enter Paoli and return to your car.

Camping along the Whitewater River

6

Morgan's Raid

60 miles; moderately hilly

Morgan's Raid, the only major Confederate raid into Indiana during the Civil War, is the main feature of this tour. The tour covers the area where Morgan ventured into Indiana, between Salem and Corydon in Washington and Harrison counties.

Morgan's Raid
by Arville L. Funk *(used with permission)*

Hoosiers of southern Indiana recall again the romance of the dashing Confederate cavalryman, John Hunt Morgan, and his celebrated raid through Indiana in July 1863. The raid itself has become a legend, and at times it seems the trails of Morgan have not changed since that warm, sultry day he crossed the Ohio River from Brandenburg, Kentucky.

The main purpose of Morgan's Raid was to divert the attention of Union forces that were threatening Confederate forces in Tennessee. Morgan's orders from General [Braxton] Bragg called only for an invasion of Kentucky. It has never been fully explained why the daring cavalry leader thought a raid across the Ohio [River] into Indiana would be more effective. Doubtless he was encouraged by knowledge that there were many southern sympathizers in Indiana from whom aid was expected.

Morgan's division was composed of some 2,500 cavalrymen. . . . As Morgan and most of the division were from Kentucky, they were welcomed with open arms through much of that state. . . . On the morning of July 8 they arrived at the small Kentucky river town of Brandenburg. Two steamers were seized, the Alice Dean and the T. J. McCombs, to transport the troops across to a point east of Mauckport [Indiana].

The crossing was interrupted by some artillery fire from a small company of the Harrison County Legion and a riverboat, the Lady Pike. When Morgan's artillery returned fire, the Lady Pike retreated, and the six-pounder on the opposite shore was silenced.

Governor Oliver P. Morton, on receiving information of the invasion of

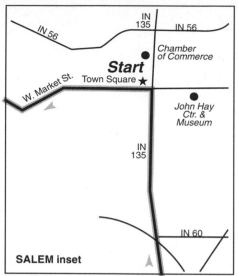

SALEM inset

IN 56
IN 135
IN 56

● Chamber
of Commerce

Start
Town Square ★

W. Market St.

● John Hay
Ctr. &
Museum

IN 135

IN 60

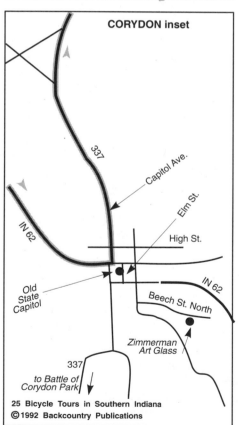

CORYDON inset

337

IN 62

Capitol Ave.

Elm St.

High St.

IN 62

Old
State
Capitol

Beech St. North

● Zimmerman
Art Glass

337

to Battle of
Corydon Park

25 Bicycle Tours in Southern Indiana
©1992 Backcountry Publications

**Tour 6:
Morgan's Raid**

◄ Direction
of travel

Start ★

IN 135
IN 56
IN 160

○ SALEM
(see
inset)

0   0.5   1.0 Mile

N

Becks Mill Rd.

○ BECKS
MILL

IN
135

○ FREDRICKSBURG

IN 150

North
Rd.

○ PALMYRA

○ HANCOCK
CHAPEL

Hancock
Chapel Rd.

CENTRAL
BARREN ○

Corydon-
Ramsey
Rd.

○ RAMSEY

IN
135

○ CORYDON
JUNCTION

NEW
SALISBURY

○ MOTTS
STATION

🛡64

CORYDON
(see inset)

IN 62

IN
135

IN 62

Indiana soil, issued a proclamation ordering all able-bodied male citizens south of the National Road [today's US 40] to form into companies and arm themselves with such arms as they could procure.

On the morning of July 9 the advance guard moved north on the Mauckport Road. One mile south of Corydon, the scouts encountered the Harrison County Home Guard (officially the Sixth Regiment of the Indiana Legion).

Numbering about 450, the home guards were drawn up in a battle line behind a hastily thrown up barricade of logs. In a short but spirited battle, Morgan met his first and only organized resistance in the Hoosier State. By outflanking both wings at the same time, Morgan's men completely routed the militia. Four of the guards were killed, several wounded, 355 captured, and the rest escaped. The victory was not without cost to the raiders; eight were killed and thirty-three wounded.

The prisoners were paroled by Morgan on entering the town of Corydon, and the raiders began collecting the spoils of victory. Most of the afternoon was spent in plundering the stores and collecting ransom money. While resting at Corydon, Morgan first learned of the fall of Vicksburg and Gettysburg from a newspaper just arrived from the north.

Late in the day the troops left Corydon and marched northward. The main column took New Salisbury, while several companies made sorties over the countryside to other villages, collecting fresh horses and plunder. During the night, bivouac was made along the road south of Palmyra for a few hours.

On the morning of July 10 the scattered [Confederate] troops reunited at Salem. Militia gathered there was easily overcome without exchange of fire. Salem suffered more from the raiders than any other town in Indiana. The men plundered in the most reckless manner, taking everything they could get their hands on, useful or not. The railway track for considerable distance was torn up, the depot and several bridges destroyed, and large ransoms demanded from the mills.

By this time, federal troops were in Palmyra, and General Hobson's Union troops numbering 6,000 were not far behind. [Indiana] Governor Morton had called in General Lew Wallace to lead a hastily organized and poorly armed militia of 3,500 south from Indianapolis (where 20,000 had mobilized) with orders "to push General Morgan through Indiana as rapidly as possible," but to avoid conflict because of the scarcity of arms.

From Salem, Morgan turned to the east. At the town of Vienna the raiders captured the railroad telegrapher. They moved on to Lexington, a larger town, then the county seat of Scott County, and camped that night in the town square.

In the morning, July 11, Morgan moved troops northward toward Vernon and North Vernon, important railway centers. Some 2,500 opposition forces had gathered at Vernon and with guns planted on high points were determined to hold the town. When Morgan sighted the organized defense, he sent forward a flag of truce demanding immediate surrender. Colonel Williams, in command of Vernon, sent back a spirited reply. Several messages were exchanged, and the women and children evacuated. Meanwhile, Morgan quietly deployed his men south and east behind cover of the hills and instead of attacking, as Williams expected, moved south toward Dupont without firing a shot.

At Dupont they got busy and repeated the work done at Vienna, seizing the telegraph station and sending out misleading messages and misinformation. The night was spent here, but early in the morning, July 12, Morgan broke camp and headed almost due east across the country to the Michigan Road. Just four hours later, Hobson's troops marched into Dupont, having come straight from Paris, while Morgan's troops were making the fruitless twenty-four-mile trip to Vernon.

Striking the Michigan Road at about Bryantsburg, Morgan led his men north to Versailles, where several hours were spent in plundering. At Osgood, a point on the vital Ohio and Mississippi Railroad, two railway bridges were destroyed and miles of track torn up. From here the raiders fled northeast through Dearborn County, rather difficult terrain, crossing into Ohio near Harrison about noon of July 13.

After fighting almost constant battles with his pursuers, Morgan and his exhausted troops were captured on July 27 in Ohio. Morgan, always the master strategist, was able to escape prison and returned to the South.

Salem is the county seat of Washington County. Platted in 1814, the town was named for Salem, North Carolina. The courthouse was built in 1888 and houses some interesting war memorabilia scattered about.

Salem is also the hometown of John Hay, author, diplomat, and Abraham Lincoln's personal secretary. His home is preserved and on display in town (see Tour 8). The town has an abundance of beautiful old homes and an interesting pre-Civil War cemetery.

0.0   START in Salem at the public parking lot at the east end of the town square on Market Street.

0.0   WEST on Market Street (circle half of the town square) and follow Market Street out of Salem.

1.0   LEFT on unmarked Beck's Mill Road, at the intersection with the sign for Colglazier Orchard.

Pass the orchard and the remnants of Beck's Mill. The mill ceased functioning about thirty-five years ago.

12.8   LEFT on IN 150, and pass through Fredricksburg (where there are no facilities).

Fredricksburg was originally called Bridgeport. Frederick Royse laid out the town in 1815, and the name was changed to honor him.

13.4   RIGHT on North Road, the first right after leaving Fredricksburg.

16.4   LEFT on Hancock Chapel Road, at Hancock Chapel.

17.5   RIGHT on Corydon-Ramsey Road.

It is the first right after turning onto Hancock Chapel Road. Pass through Ramsey (which has a restaurant and grocery).

29.2   LEFT onto IN 62 and enter Corydon.

Corydon has a restaurant, grocery, and hotels at its western edge. It served as Indiana's first state capital, from 1816-25. The town was laid out in 1807 by Harvey Heth. In 1813 the Indiana territorial capital was moved from Vincennes to Corydon. Territorial Governor William Henry Harrison named the town in honor of the shepherd Corydon from "The Pastoral Elegy."

The Old State Capitol was finished in 1816 and originally was to have served as the Harrison County Courthouse. Located on Capitol Avenue, the courthouse was preserved by the state in 1929. Between 1813 and 1816, the territorial legislature did not have a place to meet since the capital building was still under construction. During the blistering heat of the summers, the legislators met under a giant elm tree on High Street. In 1816 delegates met under this tree to write the state's first constitution. The tree was later

Traveling along the Corydon-Ramsey Rd.

named the Constitutional Elm. It died in 1925 and its trunk was preserved in 1930.

Only two battles of the Civil War were fought in the North-Gettysburg and the battle of Corydon. On July 9, 1863, Confederate General John Hunt Morgan and 2,500 calvary attacked Corydon. About a mile south of town, Corydon's Home Guard attempted to halt the invaders. After a twenty-five minute skirmish, the Home Guard were overwhelmed. Morgan and his men looted Corydon and continued north. The county has preserved the battleground as a park. It is located one mile south of town on IN Business 135, on the east side of the road.

There are a number of historic buildings and sites to see throughout the town and surrounding area. You can easily make a day of bicycling just traveling around the area. Be sure to go to the visitors' center of the Chamber of Commerce to get maps and information. It is located at 310 North Elm Street.

One place not to miss is Zimmerman Art Glass on Beech Street North. The artisans there still manufacture glass products using techniques that predate the Revolutionary War. The shop is open for tours Thursday through Sunday.

31.1   ENTER downtown Corydon.

57.5   RETURN to Salem. Head north on IN 135 and follow it all the way back to Salem.

This is the route that General Morgan took out of Corydon. You pass through several small communities as you travel north through Harrison County on IN 135, including Mott's Station, Corydon Junction, New Salisbury, and Central Barren.

At the north end of the county (13 miles north of Corydon), you enter Palmyra (which has a convenience store, restaurant, and camping). Palmyra was first settled in 1810 by Hays McCallen and was called McCallen's Cross Roads. In 1836 the town was formally laid out and renamed Carthage. Unfortunately, a town in Henry County already was using that name. In 1839, Palmyra assumed its present name.

In Palmyra is located the Buffalo Trace Park. Indians and early settlers used an old buffalo trail as a "highway" into Indiana. This old trace was used by buffalo in an annual migration from the Mississippi River to salt licks near Louisville. The ground was beaten down so heavily by the millions of hooves that it can still be clearly seen from the air. The counties established the park in 1974; it has a lake and camping facilities.

Bicycle Repair Service
Spoke & Sprocket, 108 North Main, Salem, IN 47167 (812) 883-6882.

7

Squire Boone Caverns Loop

33 miles; moderate to easy

The highlights of this tour include Corydon, a former Indiana state capital and the only town in Indiana to be attacked during the Civil War; Haysworth Nature Reserve; Boone Caverns, a spectacular cave containing onyx curtains and rare cave pearls; and Squire Boone Village, featuring a working replica mill.

This tour is a loop that you can enjoy either by itself or in conjunction with the Morgan's Raid tour(Tour 6). This tour begins in Corydon at the intersection of IN 62 and IN 135. Travel down IN 135 to Mauckport and to Squire Boone Caverns, then back up IN 135 to Corydon. Plenty of parking is available in Corydon, in public lots or along the streets.

Country road outside of Corydon

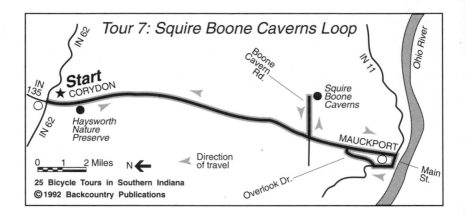

0.0   **START in Corydon at the intersection of IN 62 and IN 135.**

0.0   **LEFT (South) on IN 135, and follow it down to the Ohio River to the junction of IN 11.**

One mile outside Corydon is Haysworth Nature Reserve. This 160-acre reserve features a 40-acre forest of mixed hardwoods, a lake, hiking trails, and canoe and boat rentals on the Indian Creek.

14.2   **RIGHT on the unmarked road that runs parallel to the river, and follow it into Mauckport.**

Mauckport was laid out in 1827 and was named for Frederick Mauck, who operated a ferry across the Ohio River and made the original town plat. The town prospered as a river port and, in fact, competed for the southern terminus of the Michigan Road. Madison won out over all competing cities due to its population and economic strength. Mauckport was almost totally destroyed by the devastating flood of 1937 and has never really recovered.

14.6   **RIGHT on the main street in Mauckport, up the grade.**

15.7   **RIGHT on unmarked Overlook Drive, then back south to the Mauckport Overlook.**

16.1   **LEFT on IN 135, to signs for Squire Boone Caverns and Village.**

18.8   **RIGHT on Boone Cavern Road, and follow it to Squire Boone Caverns and Village.**

Squire Boone, Daniel Boone's brother, discovered a series of caves above the Ohio River in 1790. Fourteen years later, Squire settled near the caves and built a gristmill, the first in the area. He used the water that poured from the entrance of the caverns to power the mill. It took Boone and his sons nearly four years to build the mill. He and his family prospered with the mill. He died in 1815 and was buried in a small cave near the major cavern.

In 1972 the area was purchased by a private organization and was opened to the public the following year. The incredible formations and waterfalls inside the caverns were previously virtually impossible to reach due to the torrent of water coming from the only entrance. In 1973 new entrances were made that allowed access to the wonders of the caverns. A 48-foot mineral column, onyx curtains, and rare cave pearls are just some of the highlights you can see on the one-hour tour. (There is an admission charge; the caverns are open daily March through December and on weekends in January and February.)

The Squire Boone Village has a working replica of the mill, picnic areas, campground, an arts and craft shop, a Native American museum, and nature trails.

20.3 RETRACE the route back to IN 135.

21.8 RIGHT on IN 135, heading north.

32.5 RETURN to the intersection of IN 62 and SR 135 in Corydon.

Tour 8:
Salem-Jeffersonville Loop: Weekender

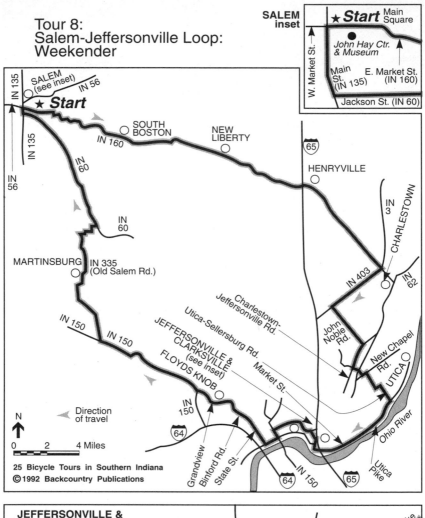

SALEM inset

★ **Start** Main Square

John Hay Ctr. & Museum

W. Market St.

Main St. (IN 135)

E. Market St. (IN 160)

Jackson St. (IN 60)

IN 135

SALEM (see inset)

IN 56

★ **Start**

IN 135

IN 56

IN 60

SOUTH BOSTON

IN 160

NEW LIBERTY

65

HENRYVILLE

IN 3

CHARLESTOWN

MARTINSBURG

IN 335 (Old Salem Rd.)

IN 60

IN 403

IN 62

IN 150

IN 150

Charlestown-Jeffersonville Rd.

Utica-Sellersburg Rd.

JEFFERSONVILLE & CLARKSVILLE (see inset)

FLOYDS KNOB

Market St.

John Noble Rd.

New Chapel Rd.

UTICA

N

Direction of travel

IN 150

64

Grandview

Binford Rd.

State St.

Ohio River

Utica Pike

0 2 4 Miles

25 Bicycle Tours in Southern Indiana
©1992 Backcountry Publications

64

IN 150

65

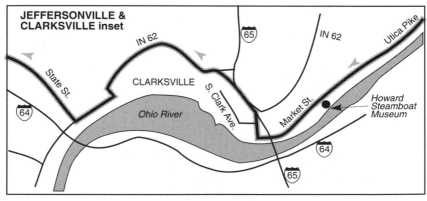

JEFFERSONVILLE & CLARKSVILLE inset

IN 62

65

IN 62

Utica Pike

State St.

64

CLARKSVILLE

S. Clark Ave.

Ohio River

Market St.

Howard Steamboat Museum

64

65

8

Salem-Jeffersonville: Weekender

48 miles one way, 82 miles round trip; moderately hilly

The highlights of this tour include Salem, the hometown and preserved home of John Hay, Lincoln's personal secretary; the "Falls" of the Ohio; Jeffersonville, the home of the *Louisville Slugger*, steamboats, and Jeffboat; a clock bigger than London's Big Ben; and Floyd's Knob, a rather unusual geological formation.

The tour starts at the public parking lot on Market Street at the east end of the main square in Salem, the county seat of Washington County. Platted in 1814, the town was named for Salem, North Carolina. The courthouse was built in 1888 and houses some interesting war memorabilia.

Salem is also the hometown of John Hay, author, diplomat, and Abraham Lincoln's personal secretary. Hay's home is preserved and on display in town. Salem has an abundance of beautiful old homes and an interesting pre-Civil War cemetery.

0.0 **EAST on East Market Street and follow it out of Salem.**
East Market Street becomes IN 160 outside Salem. Pass through the towns of South Boston, New Liberty, and Henryville on this long stretch.

32.1 **RIGHT on IN 403 at Charlestown.**
Be careful-traffic may be heavy.

35.5 **LEFT on John Noble Road.**

37.1 **RIGHT on Charlestown-Jeffersonville Road.**

41.6 **LEFT on Utica-Sellersburg Road.**
Jog left on New Chapel Road, and immediately turn right back onto Utica-Sellersburg Road. The road winds through the country to Utica (which has no facilities). Be sure to follow the road signs.

Utica was platted in 1816. The origin of its name is unknown, but it is possibly named for Utica, New York.

48.1 **RIGHT onto Fourth Street in Utica.**
The road becomes Utica Pike outside Utica, then Market Street as you enter Jeffersonville.

Jeffersonville

Jeffersonville was laid out in 1802 near a series of rapids on the Ohio River called the Falls of the Ohio. These Falls forced river traffic to portage around them, making the town's location ideal for commerce and shipping. Territorial Governor William Henry Harrison laid out the town following a plan designed by Thomas Jefferson.

Boat building was a major industry in Jeffersonville. James Howard and his descendants built steamboats in Jeffersonville from 1834 to 1848. With the death of the steamboat, the company switched to making tugboats and barges, until those operations also ceased in 1931.

One of Howard's sons built a twenty-two-room Victorian mansion in the 1890s. In 1958, the Clark County Historical Society bought the house and restored it as a museum. The Howard National Steamboat Museum is located at 1101 East Market Street. The museum has a variety of relics and displays reflecting the golden years of steamboating. The U.S. Navy bought the shipyards during World War II and produced landing craft.

Located across from the museum are the Jeffboat shipyards. Founded in 1938, Jeffboat at one time was the largest inland shipyard in the nation. Jeffboat bought the Howard shipyards from the Navy after World War II and absorbed them into its shipyard complex. Barges and towboats are the main products that Jeffboat manufactured.

The great Ohio River flood of 1937 nearly destroyed Jeffersonville. Over ninety percent of its area was flooded, and the damage was catastrophic. Jeffersonville is the home of the Hillerich, Bradsby manufacturer of the Louisville Slugger baseball bat and Powerbilt golf clubs. The firm allows visitors into the factory during normal business hours.

50.5   FOLLOW IN 62 west into Clarksville.

Clarksville was chartered in 1783 from a 150,000-acre parcel that the State of Virginia gave to George Rogers Clark for his services during the Revolutionary War. Its location was not nearly as ideal as Jeffersonville, and its growth and economy were of little significance until after World War II. Since then, Colgate-Palmolive has built a large plant in the community. In the 1920s Colgate-Palmolive bought the old Indiana Reformatory for Men and converted it to a manufacturing facility. Located on South Clark Avenue, this industrial complex features a massive forty-foot clock. It is alleged to be the second largest in the world and is actually larger than Big Ben. The clock was moved from one of Cogate's East Coast plants during the renovation of the former men's prison.

56.5   **RIGHT on State Street.**
>State Street becomes Binford Road, then Grandview. Climb Floyd's Knob on this road. Floyd's Knob is an unusual geological formation like a small plateau, with steep, rugged sides that seems to stick up out of the ground for no apparent reason.

63.0   **RIGHT on IN 150.**

72.8   **RIGHT on IN 335 (Old Salem Road).**
>Pass the town of Martinsburg. IN 335 makes several doglegs-be sure to follow signs to stay on it.

82.0   **LEFT on IN 60, and follow it into the outskirts of Salem.**

82.6   **RIGHT on IN 135, and return to the town square.**
>Nearly every major hotel/motel chain has facilities in one of these cities. Accommodations will not be a problem.

Bicycle Repair Services
Clarksville Schwinn Cyclery, 111 West Highway 131, Clarksville, IN 47130 (812) 948-2453).
Jeffersonville Schwinn, 1537 East 10th, Jeffersonville, IN 47130 (812) 284-2453.
Spoke & Sprocket, 108 North Main, Salem, IN 47167 (812) 284-2453.

Taking a break outside of Salem

9

Jackson County Loop

32 miles; moderate to easy, with a few hills

Highlights of this tour include the site of the first national train robbery; the site where the first brushless shaving cream was made; a triple burr-arched covered bridge; and the hometown of the famous rock star John "Cougar" Mellencamp.

The tour starts in Seymour. Parking is plentiful throughout the town. There is public parking just off US 50, in the heart of the business district.

Seymour

Seymour was platted in 1852 and incorporated in 1865. It prospered as the eastern terminus of the transcontinental railroad, the Chicago, Milwaukee, St. Paul and Pacific Railroad. It is also the site of the nation's first train robbery, which was perpetrated in 1866 by John and Simeon Reno and Franklin Sparks. The nation's first hanging of a train robber also occurred in Seymour, shortly after the capture of the Reno gang.

Seymour was later home to the first brushless shaving cream, Barbasol. Invented in 1918 by Seymour native Frank Brown Shields, the Barbasol Company was headquartered in Indianapolis until it was sold to the Charles Pfizer Company in 1962.

No discussion of Seymour would be complete without mentioning that it is the hometown of rock artist John "Cougar" Mellencamp. Many of the events and concepts mentioned in Mellencamp's songs derive from his youth and experiences in Seymour.

0.0   START in the parking lot on US 50 in the heart of Seymour.

0.0   WEST on IN 258 in Seymour.

3.0   CROSS Bell's Ford Covered Bridge.
This bridge is the only triple burr-arch covered bridge in Indiana.

5.5   ENTER Cortland.
Cortland was founded by Cyrus Dunham and named in honor of his hometown, Cortland, New York. The town was platted in 1842. There is a convenience store here. Leave Cortland, continuing on IN 258.

5.6   LEFT on 225E, the first paved road on the left after leaving Cortland.
Follow 225E as it jogs right, then left (don't go on the gravel roads), then becomes 200E. Eventually it curves to the right and becomes 450N.

14.6   LEFT on 25E and continue to where it crosses the White River.
It then curves to the right and becomes Base Road. You will enter Brownstown (where there is a grocery, restaurant, hotel, and camping) on Base Road. Brownstown is the county seat of Jackson County. Its courthouse, built in 1873, underwent a massive facelift in 1911. The town was named after a War of 1812 soldier, General Jacob Brown. It was platted in 1816.

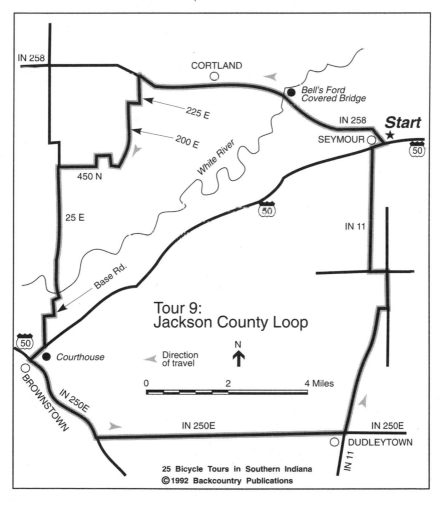

Tour 9:
Jackson County Loop

25 Bicycle Tours in Southern Indiana
©1992 Backcountry Publications

County road 225E outside of Cortland

Just off the courthouse square, on Sugar Street, is the Ball Memorial Museum. Administered by the Jackson County Historical Society, the museum contains a variety of interesting local artifacts.

14.6   LEFT (East) on IN 250E.

23.3   LEFT on IN 11 in Dudleytown.
Follow IN 11 into Seymour.

31.4   RIGHT onto US 50 in Seymour.

31.9   RETURN to the parking lot.

Bicycle Repair Service
Engelkings Bicycle Shop, 234 South O'Brien, Seymour, IN 47274 (812) 522-6045.

10

Lawrence County

52 miles; moderate with a few hills

"Don't give up the ship!" were the immortal dying words of Captain James Lawrence to his crew during the War of 1812. This route, a 52-mile loop through Lawrence County, can be split into a two-day ride if you stop over at beautiful Spring Mill State Park, which has both an inn and a campground. There are numerous attractions on this route, including a mastodon jaw, a covered bridge, caves, a pioneer village, a virgin forest, and a memorial to a space pioneer. The route is mostly rolling terrain, with no major hills. Plan on spending some time at Spring Mill State Park and enjoy its history and natural beauty.

0.0   START in Bedford, at the driveway between Golden Corral and Rax near the junction of IN 37 and IN 450.

0.0   RIGHT (West) on IN 450.

0.1   CROSS IN 37.

0.3   LEFT to follow IN 450.
Take this road into the town of Williams.

9.2   CROSS the railroad tracks and enter Williams.
Stop at the bait shop on the right. The owner has a mastodon jaw, which he found a few miles below the Williams Dam on the White River in 1988. During that year, a serious drought lowered the level of the river and exposed the jaw. You can buy a T-shirt that proudly proclaims "I Saw the Jaw."

9.2   CONTINUE on IN 450 up the hill to Pinnik's Country Store.
(which offers sandwiches, drinks, and other items).

9.3   LEFT at the top of the hill.

9.4   RIGHT at the T, back onto IN 450.

10.2   LEFT under the railroad tracks.

10.7   CROSS the White River on the Williams Covered Bridge.
The Williams Covered Bridge was built in 1884. At 376 feet, it is the longest covered bridge in the state still open to traffic.

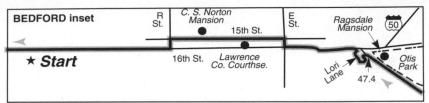

BEDFORD inset

R St.

C. S. Norton Mansion

15th St.

E St.

Ragsdale Mansion

50

★ *Start*

16th St.

Lawrence Co. Courthse.

Lori Lane

47.4

Otis Park

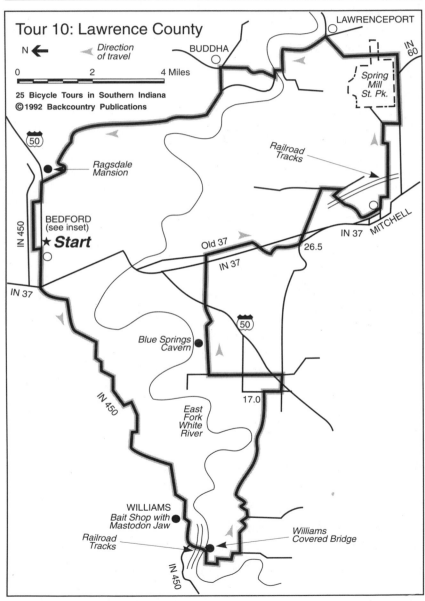

Tour 10: Lawrence County

N ←

Direction of travel

0   2   4 Miles

25 Bicycle Tours in Southern Indiana
©1992 Backcountry Publications

LAWRENCEPORT

BUDDHA

IN 60

Spring Mill St. Pk.

50

Ragsdale Mansion

Railroad Tracks

BEDFORD
(see inset)
★ **Start**

IN 450

Old 37

IN 37

26.5

IN 37 MITCHELL

IN 37

Blue Springs Cavern

50

IN 450

East Fork White River

17.0

WILLIAMS
Bait Shop with Mastodon Jaw

Railroad Tracks

Williams Covered Bridge

IN 450

12.1   **LEFT at the first opportunity.**

13.3   **LEFT at the second opportunity.**

17.0   **RIGHT at the T.**

17.5   **LEFT at the intersection.**

18.0   **CROSS US 50.**

18.0   **LEFT at the intersection.**

20.0   **CROSS US 50.**

20.1   **RIGHT at the second opportunity.**

21.6 Bluesprings Caverns is on the north side of the road. Stop and take an underground boat ride. The rides leave every hour during the summer.

Bluesprings Caverns

The East fork of the White River gradually cut its way into the limestone around Bedford thousands of years ago. The surface streams remaining on the plain above gradually seeped through the limestone, slowly dissolving the rock and eventually forming the passages that are part of Bluesprings Caverns today.

During the Ice Age, glaciers moved south across most of Indiana and deposited debris into the White River and the caverns. After the climate warmed and the glaciers retreated, water began flowing again and carried away the glacial deposits, which were fifty feet deep in some areas. The entrance to the cave was formed in the 1940s, when a farm pond, swollen by heavy rain, caused a portion of the cave's roof to collapse.

Today you can take a boat ride through the cave, accompanied by a guide who will point out the many natural features. Blind fish and blind crayfish live in the cave's waters. They have adapted to the constant 52-degree temperature and their metabolisms are lower than similar species living outside the cave. Occasionally, small fish and frogs get washed down into the cave. Unless they flow on out of the cave, they soon die because the cool temperatures cause them to become inactive. The blind fish and crayfish in the cave are scavengers, and this is their source of food.

For more information contact: Bluesprings Caverns Park, R.R. 11, Box 479, Bedford, IN 47421 (812) 279-9892. The caverns are open daily from May 1 to September 30, weekends in April and October. Cavern tours leave hourly between 9:00 and 5:00.

23.8   **RIGHT at the T, onto Old 37.**

Just 0.2 miles north of this intersection was once the national headquarters of the American Red Cross. Unfortunately, nothing remains there now except two crumbling columns that once marked the entrance. The farmland was donated to the Red Cross by a prominent local citizen, Joseph Gardener, in 1893. His third wife, Enola Lee, was an associate of Clara Barton, who founded the organization in 1881. Unfortunately, the farm was poorly managed, and tax payments were not made. The Gardeners retook possession of the property in 1904. That same year, the house on the property, which contained many Red Cross artifacts, burned down.

26.5   CROSS IN 37.

26.5   LEFT at the four-way intersection, and immediately recross IN 37.

27.9   RIGHT at the T.

The large cement factory to the left, in the distance, is the former Lehigh Portland Cement Company, which opened its first midwestern plant here in 1902. It was sold in 1979 to the Heidelberg Cement Company.

28.8   CONTINUE into Mitchell.

28.8   RIGHT at the yield sign onto Hancock.

Mitchell was originally named Mitchell's Crossing because two railroad lines intersected at this site. It is named for Ormsby McKnight Mitchell, the chief engineer of the Ohio and Mississippi Railroad, who chose the site for the tracks in 1853.

28.9   CROSS the railroad tracks.

28.9   LEFT on Seventh Street.

29.2   The Mitchell Opera House is on the right. This building was built in 1902 to hold public meetings. In 1913 it became a city hall, but by 1916, it was in such bad shape that some thought it should be demolished. Menlo Moore, a theater owner, renovated the structure and turned it into an opera house. It was used in this manner from 1919 to 1927, then became a city hall again. After the new city hall was opened in 1979, local citizens again turned it into an opera house. Today, there are frequent performances on Saturday evenings during the summer here. If you are going to spend the night at Spring Mill State Park, which is just a few miles down the road, you might wish to check the schedule to see what's playing.

29.5   LEFT on Grissom Avenue.

This road is named for Gus Grissom, one of America's original Mercury astronauts. This is the street where he grew up and where his parents still live.

29.5   RIGHT on Eighth Street, and proceed to City Hall.

29.6   The forty-four-foot high limestone monument is a replica of the

Redstone rocket that propelled Gus Grissom's Mercury capsule on its suborbital flight in 1961.

The wall around it was constructed of bricks from the elementary school Grissom attended, which formerly occupied this site. On the fins of the rocket is the tale of Grissom's life. It concludes with his words: "The conquest of space is worth the risk of human life." Grissom died along with two other astronauts while training for the first Apollo mission on January 27, 1967.

Before Grissom's elementary school occupied this site, it was home to the Southern Indiana Normal College-nicknamed SIN College by its students. Founded in 1880, it generally had more students than Indiana University. The college burned in 1900 and was never reopened.

29.6 **NORTH on Eighth Street.**
Turn around after visiting the memorial.

29.9 **RIGHT on Main Street.**
Jack's Lounge is the place for prime rib, and it attracts patrons from as far away as Louisville and Indianapolis. Bobby Knight, the Indiana University basketball coach, occasionally eats here. I asked a waitress if Knight ever threw any chairs when he visited, and she assured me he had not.

The prime rib at Jack's is large enough to easily feed two people. Before you order, ask to see the size of one. They will be glad to split an order for a dollar extra. The prime rib is not just big, it is also very tender.

30.0 **RIGHT on Fifth Street.**

30.2 **LEFT on Grissom Avenue.**

30.7 **RIGHT on Meridian Street.**

31.0 **LEFT on an unmarked road just south of Kelly Street.**
This is the last eastbound road north of IN 60.

32.4 **RIGHT at the first opportunity.**

32.8 **LEFT onto IN 60.**

33.9 **LEFT into Spring Mill State Park.**
This beautiful park has several nice trails (especially Trail 5), a restored pioneer village, the Gus Grissom Memorial, and a nature preserve of virgin timber. Plan on spending some time there.

Spring Mill State Park
During the War of 1812, when Oliver Perry defeated the British on Lake Erie, Samuel Jackson was wounded. After recovering, he served as a guide for General William Henry Harrison in the Indiana

Territory. After the war, Jackson sought a site in southern Indiana to build a gristmill. Since Spring Mill offered a steady supply of water and building materials such as limestone and timber were readily available, he built a small gristmill here in 1814.

The property was later bought by the Bullitt brothers, successful pioneer entrepreneurs who were known as "The Merchants of Louisville." The present mill was built in 1817. This impressive three-story limestone structure had a twenty-four-foot-diameter overshot wheel. A two-foot-high by four-foot-wide flume, constructed from poplar and supported by limestone piers, carried water five hundred feet to the mill. The grinding stones, made from flint, were imported from France.

The glory years of Spring Mill were from 1832 to 1872, under the management of Hugh Hamer. Until 1849, Hugh and his brother Thomas co-owned and managed the town. Business was so good that farmers often had to wait nine to ten days to get their corn ground. Whiskey was produced and marketed under the name Old Hamer. Hogs were fattened with the leftovers from the distillery and allowed to roam freely. The limestone fences around the Hamer homes and gardens were built to keep hogs out. Most of the products from Spring Mill were transported to Louisville. When oversupply drove prices down, goods were launched onto the White River, one mile north of town, and floated down to New Orleans by flatboat.

The Monon railroad line, built in 1853, passed through Mitchell instead of Spring Mill. Many of the village's major markets were lost at the outbreak of the Civil War. Steam-powered gristmills eventually put the mill out of business in 1892, and the village became a ghost town after the death of the last owner, Johnathon Turley in 1896.

Spring Mill remained dormant until it was opened as a state park in 1930. If you hike along Trail 4, you can see the limestone quarry that was used when the mill was constructed, and the flume that carries water to the mill. You may wish to browse through the pioneer village and talk to the blacksmith or some of the town's other craftsmen. Occasionally a pioneer wedding or a similar activity takes place in Spring Mill.

If you'd like to know more about this area, pick up *The Village That Slept Awhile* by Ralph L. Brooks (revised by Lois Mittino Gray). This 21-page book is available at the park and is well worth its modest price. It is highly recommended to all those with an interest in American history.

Gus Grissom State Memorial

Virgil Ivan "Gus" Grissom, one of America's original seven astronauts, was born on April 3, 1926, in Mitchell, Indiana. After graduating from high school in 1944, he served in the Air Force until he was discharged in November 1945, after the end of World War II. He enrolled at Purdue

University under the G.I. bill in 1946. After receiving his degree in mechanical engineering, he rejoined the Air Force in 1950.

During the Korean War, Grissom was a fighter pilot and flew one hundred missions, earning the Distinguished Flying Cross and the Air Medal. After returning from Korea, he spent four years at the Air Force Institute of Technology in Dayton, Ohio. His next stop was Edwards Air Force Base in California, where he was a test pilot.

When NASA announced its first seven astronauts in April 1959, Gus Grissom was among this group and was the second American to go into space, on July 21, 1961. Following his suborbital flight, the Mercury capsule, named *Liberty Bell 7*, was lost at sea.

Grissom's next trip into space was on board *Gemini 3*, the first manned Gemini flight. Along with his copilot, John Young, he completed three orbits before returning to earth. His capsule, *The Unsinkable Molly Brown*, is on display at the memorial. Although it appears antiquated to today's visitor, with its lack of digital readouts, the Gemini capsule was praised by astronauts for the convenience of its controls. Every control was readily accessible to the pilot. The capsule had the drawback of being rather cramped and was called the Gus-Mobile by other astronauts because Gus, at 5 foot 7, was the only one who could get inside and close the hatch without hitting himself on the head.

While practicing for Apollo I, Grissom was killed in a fire on January 27, 1967, along with astronauts White and Chaffee. He was buried in Arlington National Cemetery. Since he spent a great deal of time at Spring Mill State Park as a boy, it seemed an appropriate spot for a memorial in his honor. It was dedicated on July 21, 1971, ten years after his first spaceflight.

The visitor should be warned not to mention the book or the movie *The Right Stuff* here. Many people, especially around Mitchell, feel that Grissom was unfairly portrayed in both of these as a foul-mouthed womanizer whose bungling resulted in the loss of his Mercury capsule. After his Mercury flight, he was selected for the first Gemini and the first Apollo missions, which shows that the NASA hierarchy had a great deal of confidence in him.

For information about camping, write to: Spring Mill State Park, Box 376, Mitchell, IN 47446 or call the park at (812) 849-4129 For lodging, write the reservation clerk at Spring Mill Inn, Box 68, Mitchell IN 47446.

33.9   LEFT out of the park, onto IN 60.

34.0   LEFT at the first opportunity (where IN 60 turns right).

37.1   LEFT at the intersection in the small town of Lawrenceport.

39.0   RIGHT at the first opportunity.

39.1   CROSS the White River.

Somewhere along this site, prior to the Civil War, flatboats were launched on the White River. They were bound for New Orleans or other southern markets with goods from Spring Mill.

39.4   RIGHT at the second opportunity.

The first road is a gravel one along the river.

40.9   LEFT at the intersection in Buddha.

There is a small grocery store there. It is not known how the town of Buddha got its name. Some believe it was named for Budapest, the capital of Hungary. Others say it was named after a traveling salesman. Apparently, Buddha was not named after the founder of Buddhism.

Sam Bass, a famous outlaw in the Old West, was born just southwest of Buddha, along the White River, in 1851. He was orphaned during the Civil War and went to live with a nearby uncle. At age eighteen, Sam moved west to St. Louis, then Mississippi, and finally Texas. He embarked on a career of robbing banks, stage-coaches, and trains. Sam was killed at age twenty-seven during a bank holdup. His grandfather's log cabin, the Sheeks House, is part of the pioneer village in Spring Mill State Park.

47.4   On the right, in what is now Otis Park, is the Ragsdale Mansion. The stone bandstand in the park was built by unemployed stoneworkers during the Depression.

47.4   LEFT onto the road across from Otis Park, and cross the one-lane iron bridge.

47.8   RIGHT on Lori Lane.

48.2   LEFT on 16th Street.

Caution-the traffic in town may be heavy.

48.6   RIGHT on E Street.

48.7   LEFT on 15th Street.

49.0   The Lawrence County Courthouse was built in 1930. It utilizes the north wall of the previous courthouse, completed in 1872. This was done at the request of local stoneworkers, who wished to show the durability of limestone.

49.4   On the right is the C. S. Norton Mansion. Norton was one of the pioneers of Bedford's limestone industry.

49.7   LEFT on R Street.

49.7   RIGHT on 16th Street.

Ragsdale Mansion

50.9 **LEFT at the light into the Big Lots parking lot, and return to your car.**

Bicycle Repair Service
R & M Discount Bicycles, Route 1, Mitchell, IN 47446 (812) 849-4825.

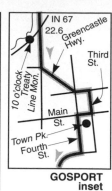

GOSPORT
inset

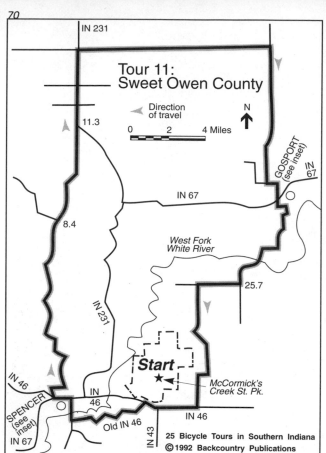

Tour 11:
Sweet Owen County

Direction of travel

N

0   2   4 Miles

IN 231

11.3

8.4

IN 231

IN 67

West Fork White River

25.7

Start

McCormick's Creek St. Pk.

IN 46

SPENCER (see inset)

IN 46

IN 67

Old IN 46

IN 43

IN 46

GOSPORT (see inset)

IN 67

25 Bicycle Tours in Southern Indiana
© 1992 Backcountry Publications

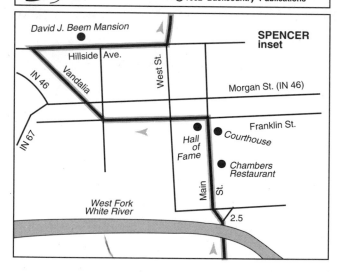

David J. Beem Mansion

SPENCER
inset

Hillside Ave.

West St.

Vandalia

IN 46

IN 67

Morgan St. (IN 46)

Franklin St.

Hall of Fame

Courthouse

Main St.

Chambers Restaurant

West Fork White River

2.5

11

Sweet Owen County

33 miles; moderate with a few hills

This ride features great scenery; sparse population; McCormick's Creek State Park; a smorgasbord; murals painted in the 1940s by Kelley, the Hobo Painter; a fur traders' gathering point (still in use); *The Spirit of the American Doughboy*; the 10 O'Clock Treaty Line Monument, a small relief sculpture; and the Owen County Hall of Fame.

While no one is exactly sure where the phrase "Sweet Owen County" originated, It is generally attributed to Dan Voorhees, a Terre Haute politician. During an election, the voting results trickled in over several days, and Voorhees trailed by a slim margin. He told his supporters that the Owen County vote would give him the victory. When his prediction came true, he said, "That's my Sweet Owen!"

Unfortunately, Owen County's roads are not too sweet. The county is sparsely populated, and is rather hilly, which makes it a great place to get away from people and enjoy beautiful scenery. But because of this, some of the roads are very rough, although they are all paved. The rolling hills are covered with woods, and many residents have built small ponds on the slopes. McCormick's Creek, Indiana's first state park, is very scenic. Plan to spend some time there and walk a few of the trails.

McCormick's Creek State Park

The park is named after John McCormick, the first white settler to lay claim to this area in 1820. The early settlers farmed and harvested timber. Attempts to build sawmills and gristmills were unsuccessful because the stream did not provide enough power. A few limestone quarries were opened, but transporting the stone across the White River to the railroad line made the operations too difficult.

Dr. Frederick Denkenwalter bought the site in 1880. He built a sanitarium on the site of the present-day Canyon Inn. The original structure had long porches on every side to offer guests a view of the picturesque surroundings.

Denkenwalter died in 1915 and the area (350 acres) was purchased by the state. As part of Indiana's centennial celebration, McCormick's Creek became the first state park, on July 4, 1916. Many of the buildings were constructed by the Civilian Conservation Corps in the 1930s. By acquiring adjacent property when it came on the market, the park has grown to its present 1,800 acres.

While you're at the park, take time to hike some of the trails. Trail 3 starts at the falls and follows the creek. Wolf Cave Nature Preserve can be visited by taking Trail 5. On this route you will pass two natural bridges. Trail 7 goes to the edge of White River and passes giant sycamores.

For information on camping, write: McCormick's Creek, Spencer, IN 47460. For hotel lodging, contact the reservation clerk at the Canyon Inn, Spencer, IN 47460 (812) 829-4881.

0.0   RIGHT out of McCormick's Creek State Park heading west on IN 41.

0.0   LEFT onto Old IN 46 (which is unmarked).

2.3   RIGHT at the T, just before the White River.

2.3   CROSS White River into Spencer.

2.5   LEFT at fork onto Main Street after crossing White River.

2.6   Chamber's Restaurant is an excellent place to eat. It has a smorgasbord for lunch and dinner and serves breakfast from a menu. It is located in the former Spencer Exchange Bank, which closed in 1929. The murals on the walls were painted in the 1940s by Kelley, the Hobo Painter. Kelley traveled about the country, trading his services in exchange for food. He also painted murals in Gosport and Cloverdale.

2.7   The Owen County Courthouse was constructed in 1909-11. After World War I, its architect, Jesse Townsend Johnson, helped redesign Arlington National Cemetery to include the Tomb of the Unknown Soldier. During the winter months, fur traders gather on the south side of the courthouse every Saturday to buy and sell pelts. This has been going on since around 1850.

On the northwest corner of the square stands the World War I monument, *The Spirit of the American Doughboy*, which was built in 1926 and was designed by Spencer native Dick Viquesney. Copies of this statue can be seen in many other places throughout the nation.

Owen County Hall of Fame

Despite the fact that Owen County has never had a large population, it has produced a number of notable people. The Owen County State Bank maintains the Owen County Hall of Fame, which is open during banking hours. Included in the hall are:

- Nellie Belles, mother of British prime minister Harold McMillan; she grew up in Spencer.

- Colonel Horace Hickman, the aviation pioneer for whom Hickman Field in Hawaii was named, was a Spencer native (Hickman Field was the initial target of the Japanese attack on Pearl Harbor).
- Ban Johnson, one of the founders of baseball's American League, who lived in Spencer and is buried in Riverside Cemetery.
- William Herschell, the poet who wrote "Ain't God Good to Indiana," and was a Spencer native.
- T. C. Steele, famous Hoosier artist (see Brown County Ride), was born in Owen County.
- James H. "Babe" Pierce, who played Tarzan in some of the early movies, was born in the nearby small town of Freedom.
- Samuel Ralston, a former governor of Indiana, grew up in nearby Patricksburg.

2.8   LEFT on Franklin Street.

3.0   BEAR RIGHT onto Vandalia.

3.3   ACUTE RIGHT onto Hillside Avenue.

> 3.4   At the top of the hill, to the left, is the David J. Beem Mansion. Captain Beem, a Civil War veteran, built this home in 1874 to resemble the homes of the South he had admired. The brick structure has four porches and fourteen-foot-high ceilings.

3.7   LEFT on West Street.

8.4   BEAR RIGHT.

11.3   CONTINUE straight onto IN 231.

13.2   RIGHT at the third opportunity.
This road is quite rough.

18.3   RIGHT at the T.

21.9   LEFT at the T.

> 22.6   At the intersection of this road and IN 67 is the 10 O'Clock Treaty Line Monument, a small relief sculpture by Spencer artist Frederick L. Hollis. It depicts Chief Little Turtle and Territorial Governor William Henry Harrison meeting at Fort Wayne. By terms of their treaty, the United States bought nearly three million acres at three cents apiece. This was called the 10 O'Clock Treaty because the boundary line followed the shadow cast by a spear stuck in the ground at ten o'clock. Surveyors of this line often had to stick a spear in the ground to prove to suspicious Indians that they were not

cheating. Gosport, which you are about to enter, is the only town lying directly on top of this line.There is also an historical marker here for Camp Hughes, a Civil War training camp used by the 59th Indiana Infantry during 1961 and 1962. The actual site of the camp was south of Gosport and along the White River.Notice that the volunteer fire station across the road is actually a converted gas station.

22.8   BEAR LEFT on Greencastle Highway.

23.1   RIGHT on Third Street.

23.2   RIGHT on Main Street.

23.2   On your left is the town park. Gosport once aspired to be the county seat, and space was left for a courthouse. When it became apparent that Spencer was going to remain the county seat, this space was turned into a park.

23.3   LEFT on Fourth Street.

23.5   RIGHT on East Goss Street.

24.0   Walk your bike across the bridge over the railroad tracks to avoid getting your wheels caught between the planks.

25.7   CROSS the White River.

25.7   RIGHT at the first opportunity after crossing the river.

26.7   LEFT at the first opportunity.

31.1   RIGHT on IN 46.

Sculpture depicting historic meeting

12

The River of Long Fish

77 miles; moderate with a few hills

This tour features the River of Long Fish; the state's highest railroad trestle; a small portion of what was once the largest deciduous tree in the nation; an Elvis impersonator who is also mayor; Shakamak State Park; and the former population center of the United States.

The tour can be split into a two-day camping/inn tour. Ride 36 miles the first day and 41 miles the second, camping overnight at Shakamak State Park; or do 49 miles the first day and 28 the second, staying at the Park Inn in Linton. (For information, call the Park Inn at (812) 847-8631.)

The tour starts at Bloomfield, the county seat of Greene County, and travels northwest to Shakamak State Park, an excellent place to camp for the night. *Shakamak* is a Kickapoo Indian word that means "River of Long Fish." "Long Fish" refers to eels, which the Indians considered a delicacy. Today the park offers good bass fishing, but very few eels remain.

Farming and coal mining are the main activities in Greene County. All roads on this route are paved, but a few have some rough spots. At several points along this route, it is necessary to take state highways. Traffic count maps indicate that they are lightly traveled, but use caution, especially if riding at peak times.

0.0   START at the Greene County Courthouse.

0.0   NORTH on IN 157.

3.3   RIGHT on 325N.

5.5   RIGHT at the T.

6.9   RIGHT at 410E.

7.6   At 480E is the state's highest railroad trestle, to the right. Almost a half-mile long, it rises to as much as 157 feet above the valley floor. It was constructed in 1905-1906 by Italian immigrant labor. Locally, rumors flew that its construction would cause one death per day. The project was completed with no fatalities at a cost of $1.5 million. To get a closer look, travel down the gravel road about a half-mile to the base of the trestle. Then return to IN 157 by the same route.

11.2   RIGHT on IN 157, into Worthington.

This town was founded when plans were made for the Central Canal to pass through the site. The canal was intended to link with the

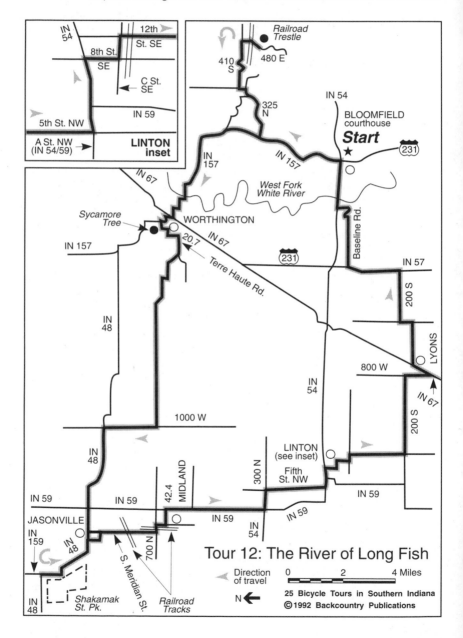

LINTON
inset

Railroad
Trestle

BLOOMFIELD
courthouse
Start
★

West Fork
White River

Sycamore
Tree

WORTHINGTON

Terre Haute Rd.

Baseline Rd.

IN 57

LYONS

IN 67

IN 54

LINTON
(see inset)

Fifth
St. NW

IN 59

JASONVILLE
IN
159

MIDLAND

S. Meridian St.

Railroad
Tracks

Shakamak
St. Pk.

IN
48

Tour 12: The River of Long Fish

Direction
of travel

N

0   2   4 Miles

25 Bicycle Tours in Southern Indiana
©1992 Backcountry Publications

Wabash and Erie Canal on both ends and pass through Indianapolis. Along much of its route, the canal was to parallel the White River. Because of financial problems, the Central Canal was never built.

18.7   RIGHT, to stay on IN 157.

18.7   LEFT, to stay on IN 157.

18.7   LEFT, to stay on IN 157. This becomes Main Street.

19.1   RIGHT on Dayton Street.

19.3   Here at the city park is a small portion of what was once the largest deciduous tree in the nation. This sycamore tree grew just south of Worthington and became a tourist attraction after it appeared on a postcard in 1911. It was 150 feet tall, had a spread of 100 feet, and was 43 feet in circumference at the base. The tree was blown down in a storm in 1920. The section in the park is only part of a limb, not the trunk. After you visit the tree, retrace your path along Dayton Street.

19.5   RIGHT onto Main Street.

19.6   LEFT at the first stop sign.

19.7   RIGHT immediately.

19.8   LEFT on Wabash Avenue.

20.0   RIGHT on Terre Haute Road.

20.7   RIGHT at the Y (stay on the paved road).

28.0   RIGHT on 1000W.

30.2   LEFT on IN 48.

33.5   ENTER Jasonville.

Jasonville is best known for being the gateway to Shakamak State Park and for having an Elvis impersonator as mayor. Camping is available at the park: write to Shakamak State Park, Route 2, Jasonville, IN 47438, or call (812) 665-2158. The Sea Cove, which will be on the left in downtown Jasonville, is a good place to eat. Continue through town on IN 48.

Mayor Elvis
Since Jasonville looks like a typical small midwestern town, it is difficult to imagine how an Elvis impersonator could become mayor. After sifting through newspaper articles in *The Jasonville Leader* and *The Linton Daily Citizen*, his rise to power can now be explained.

Mud-slinging campaigns have become way too common

A LIMB FROM THE BIG SYCAMORE TREE THAT GREW
IN WHITE RIVER BOTTOMS ABOUT 1½ MI. EAST OF
WORTHINGTON AND WAS PLACED IN THE PARK IN 1925.
IN 1915 THE AGE OF THE TREE WAS ESTIMATED TO BE
500 YR., HEIGHT 150 FT. AND THE SPREAD 100 FT.
CIRCUMFERENCE 1 FT. ABOVE GROUND WAS 45 FT. 3 IN.
CIRCUMFERENCE 5 FT. ABOVE GROUND WAS 42 FT. 3 IN.
EAST BRANCH 27 FT. 8 IN. WEST BRANCH 23 FT. 3 IN.

Sycamore Tree

across America, including Jasonville, Indiana. When Bruce Borders, an insurance agent and Elvis impersonator, was running for mayor, his opponent would hold up a picture of him and ask "Can you imagine Elvis for mayor?" This negative campaigning apparently backfired, since Borders won by eight votes, even though only 140 of the 1,105 voters were Republicans.

Borders began impersonating Presley at age seventeen, while detasseling corn during the summer. Crew members would bribe him with Twinkies to get him to sing. When Elvis died the following summer, Bruce was asked to do a local tribute. His worst nightmare came true when he forgot the words to a song during his first performance. He then dropped the act for several years before starting again.

After his election in November of 1987, WISH-TV did a human interest piece about Borders for the local news. CBS aired the piece nationwide. Since then Borders has appeared on *Late Night with David Letterman.* (Letterman's grandparents lived in nearby Linton.) Numerous radio stations have called him for interviews. One from New Zealand asked him to sing "Tie Me Kangaroo Down Sport" as Elvis would have sung it

Indiana University rock 'n' roll history professor Glenn Glass offered this analysis: "It just shows how times have changed. Thirty years ago Elvis was a dangerous threatening rebel. . . . Imagine an Elvis impersonator in 1958. He couldn't get elected to anything."

36.5 **ENTER Shakamak State Park from IN 48, on the left.**

36.5 **TURN right onto IN 48 to leave Shakamak State Park.**

38.1 **RIGHT on Fry Street as you reenter Jasonville.**

38.7 **LEFT on West Shanklin Street.**

39.4 **RIGHT on South Meridian Street.**

41.4 **LEFT on 700N.**

41.7 **RIGHT at the split after crossing the railroad tracks.**

41.9 **LEFT into the town of Midland.**

42.4 **RIGHT onto IN 59 in Midland.**

46.2 **LEFT on 300N.**

47.0 **RIGHT at the first opportunity. This becomes Fifth Street NW in Linton.**

49.2 **LEFT onto A Street NW.**
This is downtown Linton, the largest town in Greene County. From 1930 to 1940 it was the center of the United States population,

which has now moved westward toward St. Louis. It is also the hometown of Phil Harris, a well-known band leader who appeared on Jack Benny's show for many years. Every year, the Phil Harris Celebrity Golf Tourney is held the weekend after the Indianapolis 500. It attracts celebrities such as Bob Knight (Indiana University basketball coach), Chris Schenkel (ABC sportscaster), and Denny Crum (University of Louisville basketball coach). The city course has been named in honor of Phil Harris.

50.0   **RIGHT onto Eighth Street SE.**

50.2   **LEFT onto C Street SE (just before the railroad tracks).**

50.4   **RIGHT at the T onto 12th Street SE. You are leaving Linton.**

50.9   **LEFT at the T.**

51.2   **RIGHT at the first opportunity.**

53.2   **LEFT onto 200S.**

56.4   **RIGHT onto 800W.**

65.8   **LEFT at the first opportunity. This road becomes IN 67 in Lyons.**

66.6   **CONTINUE STRAIGHT when IN 67 bends left in Lyons.**

68.2   **LEFT at the T.**

68.6   **RIGHT onto 200S.**

70.6   **LEFT onto IN 57.**

72.6   **RIGHT onto Baseline Road.**

75.1   **LEFT just before IN 231 onto the entrance ramp for IN 231.**

76.9   **RETURN on IN 231 to the Greene County Courthouse.**
          The Greene County Courthouse was constructed in 1886 at a cost of $60,000.

13

Terre Haute

36 miles; moderately easy

This tour passes such sites as Paul Dresser's Home; the Sheldon Swope Art Gallery; the Rose Hulman Institute of Technology; the Markle Mill home; the home of Eugene Debs; the Hulman Center, once the home court of Larry Bird; and St. Mary of the Woods College.

While he was marching northward to the Battle of Tippecanoe in 1811, Governor William Henry Harrison built a fort a few miles north of what is now the downtown area of Terre Haute. Terre Haute was built by a group of land speculators, including the Bullitt brothers, who once owned the town of Spring Mill (see Tour 10). By donating eighty lots and $4,000, they were able to get Terre Haute named the county seat. After this, the town grew at a rapid pace. Terre Haute has always had many transportation links. It is situated on the Wabash River; the National Road (now US 40) reached town in 1835. The Wabash and Erie Canal arrived in 1849 and the Terre Haute and Richmond Railroad came in 1852.

Today, many sites here are named for two of Terre Haute's wealthiest citizens: Chauncey Rose, who made his money in the railroads, and Tony Hulman, who owned the Indianapolis Motor Speedway for many years.

0.0   **START at Paul Dresser's Home in Fairbanks Park.**
Paul Dresser wrote many songs, including "On the Banks of The Wabash," Indiana's state song. His brother, Theodore Dreiser (yes, they spelled their names differently), was an author whose best-known work is *An American Tragedy*. The house was moved to its present location in 1963.

0.0   **NORTH through the park on Dresser Drive.**
The ground for Fairbanks Park was donated by Crawford and Edward Fairbanks in memory of their father, Henry Fairbanks, who was mayor during the 1870s.

0.3   The Chauncey Rose Memorial, on your right, consists of the front of the old Federal Building.

0.8   **EXIT the park eastbound on Ohio Street.**

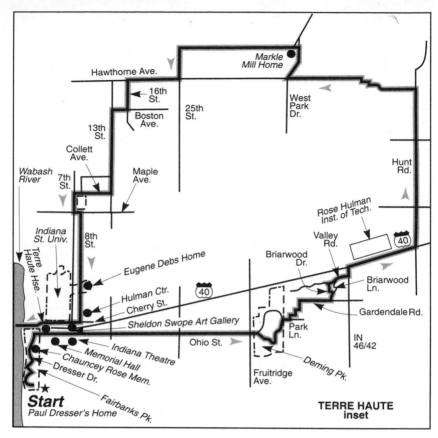

Hawthorne Ave.

Markle
Mill Home

16th
St.

West
Park
Dr.

Boston
Ave.

25th
St.

13th
St.

Collett
Ave.

Hunt
Rd.

Maple
Ave.

7th
St.

Wabash
River

Indiana
St. Univ.

Terre
Haute
Hse.

8th
St.

Rose Hulman
Inst. of Tech.

Valley
Rd.

40

Eugene Debs Home

Briarwood
Dr.

Briarwood
Ln.

Hulman Ctr.

Cherry St.

40

Gardendale Rd.

Sheldon Swope Art Gallery

Ohio St.

Park
Ln.

IN
46/42

Indiana Theatre

Memorial Hall

Chauncey Rose Mem.

Dresser Dr.

Deming Pk.

Fruitridge
Ave.

Start

Paul Dresser's Home

Fairbanks Pk.

TERRE HAUTE
inset

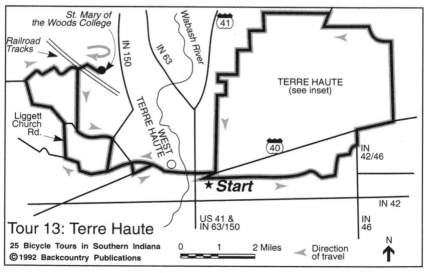

St. Mary of
the Woods College

Wabash
River

41

Railroad
Tracks

IN 150

IN 63

TERRE HAUTE
(see inset)

Liggett
Church
Rd.

WEST
TERRE
HAUTE

40

IN
42/46

★ **Start**

IN 42

Tour 13: Terre Haute

IN
46

25 Bicycle Tours in Southern Indiana
© 1992 Backcountry Publications

0   1   2 Miles

US 41 &
IN 63/150

Direction
of travel

N

0.9   Memorial Hall, on the right, is the oldest building in Terre Haute.

1.3   On the south side of the street is the Indiana Theater. This beautiful 1,660-seat theater was built in 1922 at a cost of $750,000.
On the north side is the Sheldon Swope Art Gallery. Sheldon Swope operated a jewelry store at this location. When he died in 1929, his will stipulated that a public art gallery be created.

3.9   CROSS Fruitridge Avenue into Deming Park and bear right.

4.1   RIGHT at the split in the road.

4.5   RIGHT at the first opportunity (near the tennis courts).
This lane leads to a gate that is always closed, but you can walk your bike around it.

4.6   RIGHT after walking your bike around the gate.

4.6   LEFT at the first opportunity.

4.8   LEFT on Park Lane. Go left when Park Lane splits.

5.0   RIGHT at the T onto Gardendale Road.

5.6   LEFT on Briarwood Lane.

5.7   LEFT at the split onto Briarwood Drive.

5.8   RIGHT onto Valley Road.

6.1   LEFT at the T onto IN 46.

6.3   RIGHT at the T onto US 40.

6.8   The Rose Hulman Institute of Technology is one of the nation's finest engineering schools. Chauncey Rose founded the school in 1874, and Tony Hulman, Sr., donated 123 acres for a new campus in 1917. Tony Hulman, Jr., donated the assets of the Hulman Foundation in 1971.

7.3   LEFT at the first opportunity after Rose Hulman. There is a flashing yellow light at this intersection.

7.9   Hawthorn Park offers camping.

9.4   The historical marker commemorates a stop on the Underground Railroad, which took runaway slaves to Canada and freedom.

9.7   LEFT at the third opportunity.

11.8   RIGHT at West Park Drive.

12.3   The Markle Mill home is on the left, and the dam is on the right.

Abraham Markle, one of the entrepreneurs who founded Terre Haute, built a dam and mill on this site in 1816. His son built the present home in 1848. The mill burned in 1938, and afterward the dam was neglected and began to deteriorate. Through donations and volunteer efforts, it has since been restored.

12.3   LEFT at T.

14.1   LEFT onto 25th Street, the first street after the stoplight.

14.6   RIGHT on Hawthorne Avenue.

15.3   LEFT on 16th Street.

15.7   RIGHT at the T onto Boston Avenue.

16.0   LEFT at the T onto 13th Street.

17.3   RIGHT on Collett Avenue.

17.8   LEFT at the T onto Seventh Street.

18.0   LEFT on Maple Avenue.

18.1   RIGHT on Eighth Street.

19.5   The Eugene Debs Home is located on the campus of Indiana State University. Debs was a labor leader and five-time presidential candidate for the Socialist Party.

19.8   The Hulman Center was once the home court of Larry Bird when he played for the Indiana State Sycamores. The street leading to the building has been named for him. Larry led his team to the final game of the 1979 NCAA basketball tournament, where they were beaten by Magic Johnson and the Michigan State Spartans.

19.9   RIGHT onto Cherry Street, which runs into US 40.
The Terre Haute House, a hotel, was built by Chauncey Rose.

20.4   The present Vigo County Courthouse, on the left, was built in 1888. The county is named for Francis Vigo, who loaned money to George Rogers Clark during the American Revolution. He wished to purchase a bell for the original courthouse but lacked funds because the government refused to repay his loans. When his heirs were compensated after he died in 1836, they donated money to help purchase a bell for the current courthouse.

21.6   CROSS the Wabash River.

21.6   CONTINUE straight into West Terre Haute as US 40 angles left.

24.2   RIGHT on Liggett Church Road.

Church of the Immaculate Conception

25.2   LEFT at the T.

26.9   RIGHT at the T.

28.3   LEFT at the T, and go under the railroad tracks.

28.4   RIGHT at the stop sign.
        (There is a general store if you go 0.1 miles left instead of right.)

28.8   LEFT into St. Mary of the Woods College.
        Founded in 1840, this is Indiana's oldest college for women. The
        campus has many beautiful buildings, but be sure to visit the
        Church of the Immaculate Conception. Its interior and stained glass
        windows are gorgeous.

28.8   RIGHT after viewing the campus.

29.2   LEFT at the T.

29.4   LEFT at the T after passing under the railroad tracks.

31.3   LEFT at the stop sign.

**32.4   RIGHT after passing the old school. This is the second right; the first
        has a NO OUTLET sign.**

33.1   LEFT at the stop sign.

34.2   LEFT onto US 40.

35.6   CROSS the Wabash River.

35.6   ACUTE RIGHT onto Dresser Road and into Fairbanks Park.

36.5   RETURN to Paul Dresser's Home.

Restaurant and Hotel
Larry Bird's Boston Connection.

Bicycle Repair Service
Frank's Cycle Center, 121 North 13th Street, Terre Haute, IN 47807 (812) 234-
    7731.

14

Cataract Falls

55 miles; moderate

This tour features Cataract Falls, the highest falls in the state; a bank that was robbed by the infamous John Dillinger; the only German World War II buzz bomb on public display in the United States; a historical marker commemorating the Eli Lilly-operated pre-Civil War drugstore; and DePauw University, one of the finest small liberal arts colleges in the nation.

This tour passes through Putnam, Owen, and Clay counties. It is structured to be a one-day ride out of Lieber State Recreation Area in Owen County. But it can be made into a two-day camping tour by starting in Greencastle in Putnam County, 38 miles into the tour. The rider would start in Greencastle, follow the last half of the tour (17 miles), camp at Lieber, then ride the first half of the tour (38 miles) the next day, returning to Greencastle.

0.0 START at Lieber State Park.

0.0 RIGHT (south) on IN 243.

2.5 LEFT onto IN 42.

6.5 CONTINUE straight, leaving IN 42.

7.2 RIGHT at the first opportunity.

10.3 RIGHT at the first intersection.

> 12.1 Cataract Falls State Recreation Area is on the right. The Upper Falls are the highest (45 feet) in the state, except for some that have virtually no water going over them (such as at Clifty Falls State Park). The covered bridge was built in 1876. This area was originally purchased by Theodore Jennings, brother of Indiana governor Jonathan Jennings, in 1842.

12.6 RIGHT on West Cataract Road, or continue just past it to the Cataract General Store.

> The store makes sandwiches and has plenty of munchies and drinks.

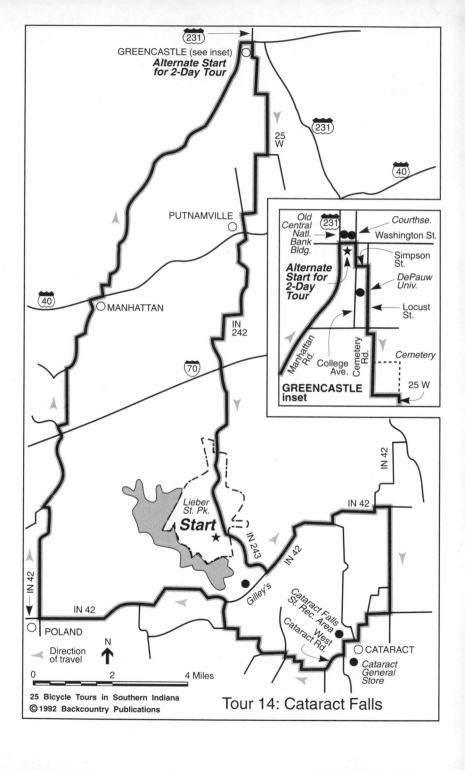

Tour 14: Cataract Falls

25 Bicycle Tours in Southern Indiana
©1992 Backcountry Publications

15.0   BEAR RIGHT.

16.5   BEAR RIGHT.

17.3   LEFT onto IN 42.
(For food, turn right onto IN 42 and eat at Gilley's, which is just up the road about a mile. It's run by Bill, not Mickey Gilley. Bill does have an autographed picture of Mickey on display, though.)

22.2   RIGHT at the first opportunity in the town of Poland.

25.0   BEAR RIGHT.

27.0   RIGHT, after passing over US 70.

28.3   BEAR RIGHT.

30.8   RIGHT on US 40 in the town of Manhattan.

30.9   LEFT at the first opportunity.
Follow this road into downtown Greencastle, where the road name becomes Manhattan Road, then Jackson Street.

38.2   RIGHT on Washington Street.
The alternate starting point for this tour is at the corner of Washington and Jackson streets in Greencastle, to make this a two-day camping tour.

The Old Central National Bank Building at the corner of Washington and Jackson was robbed by Dillinger and his gang in 1933. The Putnam County Courthouse, on your left, was built in 1905. At the southwest corner is an actual German buzz bomb from World War II, the only one on public display in the United States. On the southeast corner of the courthouse square is a historical marker commemorating the fact that Eli Lilly operated a drugstore here before the Civil War. The pharmaceutical company he later founded has its world headquarters in Indianapolis and is now a major corporation.

38.4   RIGHT on College Avenue.

38.7   LEFT onto Simpson Street, when College Avenue becomes one-way north.

38.8   RIGHT at the first opportunity, onto Locust Street.
You are riding through the campus of DePauw University, one of the finest small liberal arts colleges in the nation. It was originally named Indiana Asbury College when founded in 1837. The college was rescued from financial straits by a New Albany businessman and renamed in his honor in 1884.

39.3   RIGHT onto Cemetery Road at the T.
Cemetery Road becomes 25W after the cemetery.

41.3   RIGHT at the T.

44.4   LEFT at the T.
After crossing US 40 at Putnamville, this road becomes IN 243, which leads back to Lieber State Park.

55.3   RIGHT into Lieber State Park.
The recreation area is named for Colonel Richard Lieber, the founder of the Indiana state park system. The first state park was McCormick's Creek, which was dedicated in Indiana's centennial year, 1916.

Cataract Falls

15

The Edge of the Glacier

27 miles: easy north of the glacier line and rugged south of it

The highlight of this tour, which takes you through parts of Johnson and Brown counties, is the striking changes in the countryside caused by an ancient glacier at its southernmost line. You will see it with your eyes and feel it in your heart—and legs.

Like most of the Midwest, Indiana was once covered by a series of glaciers. These glaciers flattened everything in their path by pushing great mounds of debris in front of them, filling in all the low spots. As the glaciers receded during the warmer periods, great ravines, lakes, and rivers were carved by the melting ice. Glaciers covered the northern half of the state, stopping just south of Indianapolis.

This tour shows the results of the incredible power and strength of these huge glaciers. The tour begins in the flat farmlands of Indiana, and within five miles is transformed into the rugged, hilly, challenging course through the debris left by the retreating glaciers.

The tour begins at the Trafalgar Square Shopping Center in Trafalgar. The shopping center is at the intersection of IN 135 and IN 252.

Trafalgar was named after the 1805 British naval victory over the French and Spanish at Trafalgar, on the southwestern coast of Spain. It was originally called Liberty when it was platted in 1851. Two years later, its name was changed to Hensley Town. Finally, in 1867, it received its present name.

0.0   **LEFT (North) from the Trafalgar Square Shopping Center onto IN 135.**

0.2   **RIGHT on Pearl Street.**

0.9   **RIGHT on 225W, and immediately jog left onto Red Gold Drive.**

1.5   **RIGHT on 150W. Cross IN 252.**

3.0   **LEFT on 550S.**

4.0   **RIGHT on 50W.**
        The road curves to the left at a dead end sign and becomes 600S.

4.5   **RIGHT on Nineveh Road.**

5.7   **RIGHT on 700S.**

6.9   **LEFT on Center Line Road.**

7.8   **RIGHT on 750S.**

9.0   **LEFT on Peoga Road.**

   Peoga Road twists and curves around the perimeter of Peoga Lake.
   Be careful of oncoming traffic when rounding the narrow curves.
   The road ends at the settlement of Peoga.

   Peoga was established in 1898 when a post office was established
   to serve the area. The origin of the name is not known, but it is
   speculated to be of Native American origin.

10.3   **RIGHT on 250W at the convenience store.**

10.4   **LEFT on 900S, and follow it to Spearsville.**

13.2   **RIGHT at a three-way stop in Spearsville, onto unmarked 500W.**

16.0   **LEFT on 700S to the edge of Morgantown. (Follow 700S on into
           Morgantown for refreshments and food.)**

18.5   **RIGHT on 800W. Cross IN 135/252.**

19.5   **RIGHT on 600S.**

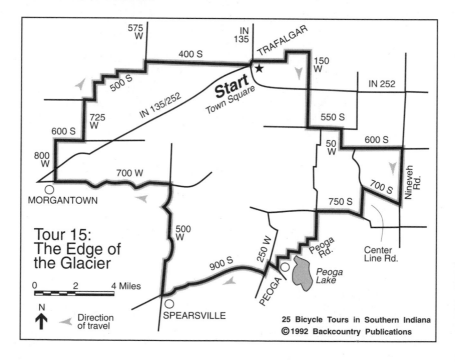

Tour 15:
The Edge of
the Glacier

0   2   4 Miles

N
Direction
of travel

25 Bicycle Tours in Southern Indiana
© 1992 Backcountry Publications

Cyclists on 900 S near Spearsville—The Edge of the Glacier

20.4   LEFT on 725W.

21.3   RIGHT on 500S.
    The road makes several 90-degree dogleg turns and eventually
    becomes 575W. Be sure to consult the map.

23.7   RIGHT on 400S and follow it back into Trafalgar.

26.4   RIGHT on IN 135, and return to Trafalgar Square Shopping Center.

16

Brown County

36 miles; hilly, with several short steep hills. (If you can ride the hill in the park up to the campground, then you can ride Indiana.)

Scenery, and lots of it, is the main feature of this tour. However, it also features food, hiking, artists, funny-paper characters, camping, panning for gold, shopping, John Dillinger, a great little store, a town called Beanblossom, and a place called Stone Head.

Consider camping in Brown County State Park, or staying at the Abe Martin Lodge, located within the park. Abe Martin was a cartoon character who appeared in the *Indianapolis News* from 1904 to 1930 and supposedly lived in Brown County. If you like hiking, the trails through Ogle Hollow Nature Preserve and around Ogle Lake are very nice. On sunny spring days, turtles like to sun themselves at the east end of the lake.

You may want to spend some time in the shops of Nashville. Brown County has long been a popular place for artists, and many sell their work in Nashville. C. Carey Cloud, a Nashville artist, designed many of the toys found in boxes of Cracker Jack. One of the more unique places is the John Dillinger Museum. Dillinger was born about 30 miles north of here, in Mooresville.

0.0   **START at the fire tower in Brown County State Park.**

0.0   **Leave the park by going left (south) through the Horseman's Campground.**

There may be some signs that say "Horsemen Only," but the guards let bicyclists pass.

2.5   **LEFT on IN 135.**

4.2   **LEFT to stay on IN 135.**

On the right is Stone Head, a distance marker that gives the mileage to nearby towns (two of which no longer exist). Carved from sandstone by Henry Cross, a part-time tombstone carver, it is a likeness of George Summa, the township road supervisor in 1851. State law at that time required all men to spend six days each year working on roads or waterways. Cross was allowed to create this road marker instead.

9.1   **LEFT on IN 46.**
Caution: There may be heavy traffic.

9.8   **RIGHT on Salt Creek Road.**
Take this road to Gatesville.

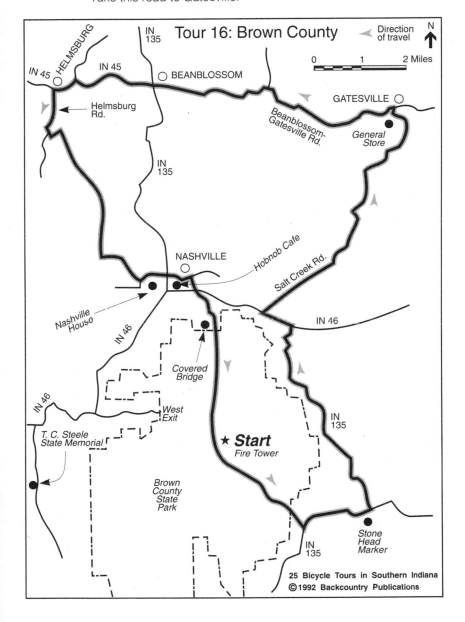

16.7   ENTER Gatesville

Gatesville consists of a general store (they sell sandwiches), a fire department, and a roadside park. Bill Gates traveled the northern portion of the Salt Creek valley in his huckster wagon many years ago. When refrigeration put an end to the huckster business, the Gatesville General Store began operations in 1915.

Today the store serves local residents and the many tourists who visit Brown County. The store still has a hitching post where horses can be tied while their riders order sandwiches and drinks. The store sells picnic supplies, deli sandwiches, freshly squeezed lemonade, pizzas (weekends after five o'clock only), and gold pans. Visitors can relax at the picnic tables in the Gatesville Roadside Park, just across the road.

During the Ice Age, glaciers brought gold from Eastern Canada to the Salt Creek valley. Gold has been mined on a small scale in Brown County ever since the mid-1800s. You can try your luck along Salt Creek, but don't expect to strike it rich. Since the gold is a glacial deposit, there is no mother lode to find. A commercial mining company was formed in 1983 when the price of gold was high.

Food and supplies: Gatesville General Store (812) 988-0477.

16.7   LEFT at the T, onto the Beanblossom-Gatesville Road.

There is no sign.

18.1   LEFT at the T.

Ride on into Beanblossom, which is the site of Bill Monroe's annual bluegrass festival, held in September. There is a store in town.

23.0   CONTINUE STRAIGHT across IN 135.

(The road is now US 45.)

24.9   LEFT at the T, to stay on US 45.

This road goes into Helmsburg, which has a small general store.

25.5   ACUTE LEFT onto Helmsburg Road.

Cross the railroad tracks, and pass the former Cullum Broom and Mop Company.

26.5   LEFT at first opportunity (to stay on Helmsburg Road).

29.7   LEFT at the T (to stay on Helmsburg Road).

Take this road straight into Nashville. You may wish to lock your bike near the town hall and wander around on foot. The Nashville House is famous for its fried biscuits and apple butter, and the Hobnob Cafe is another good place to eat. Both are at the intersection of Helmsburg Road and IN 135. The Hobnob is located in Nashville's oldest commercial building.

31.4   CROSS IN 135.

Stone head

33.6 CROSS IN 46 into Brown County State Park.

Cross Indiana's oldest covered bridge (built at a different location in 1838) and the only one with two lanes.

36.1 CONTINUE STRAIGHT up the hill to the fire tower.

(If you have sufficiently low gearing.) Just keep repeating to yourself, "Indiana is flat, Indiana is flat. . . ."

T. C. Steele Memorial

West of Nashville on IN 46 is the T. C. Steele Memorial (812) 988-2785, which commemorates artist T. C. Steele. It is a wonderful place to visit to see where he lived and worked, and to view some of his vivid landscapes.

To get there, head west on IN 46 out of Nashville. A road on the left leads to the memorial. Watch for the signs. Unfortunately, it is somewhat dangerous to visit the Steele memorial by bicycle. IN 46 is a heavily traveled, high-speed, two-lane highway with little or no shoulder. At this time it is recommended that you visit the memorial by car. Perhaps in the future the state will add a shoulder to the road so it can be reached safely by bicycle.

Theodore Clement Steele was born near Gosport in 1847. His family moved to Waveland, Indiana, where the Waveland Academy was located. His artistic skills were recognized when he was still quite young. Between 1863 and 1870, he earned his living by painting portraits, and in 1873 he moved to Indianapolis to exploit its larger portrait market there. During the severe depression that struck in 1873, he worked as a sign painter along with Hoosier poet James Whitcomb Riley (see Tour 24).

Steele secured sponsorship from several prominent Hoosiers to study at the Royal Academy in Munich, Germany, in 1880. The paintings he sent back from Europe were well received, and his patrons provided money for him to continue his work there until 1885.

After his return from Munich, Steele continued to do portraits for money, but his real passion had become landscapes. Searching for new landscapes, he bought two hundred acres in Brown County in 1907, land that is now the T. C. Steele State Memorial.

Originally Steele maintained a studio in Indianapolis for the cold winter months and used his Brown County studio during the summer. As time went on, he used the Brown County studio more and more. Eventually the grounds contained a home, studios, and several guest cottages.

After 1914, Steele's paintings generally contained no people or animals. He was striving for pure landscape. He died in 1926, and the state memorial that bears his name preserves his house, two studios, and a guest house, including a large collection of his drawings and paintings.

Tourist Information

Abe Martin Lodge (inside Brown County State Park), Reservation Clerk, Box 25, Nashville,IN 47448 (812 988-4418).

Brown County Convention and Visitor Bureau, P.O. Box 840, Nashville, IN 47448.

Brown County State Park, Nashville, IN 47448.

Division of Historic Preservation, Department of Natural Resources, 202 North Alabama Street, Indianapolis, IN 46204 (317) 232-1637.

17

Columbus-Hope Loop

38 miles; flat and easy

This is a delightful tour of Columbus, famous for its modern architecture. Then the tour ventures to Hope, a small town founded by Moravians in 1830.

The tour starts at the Columbus Visitor's Center, at Fifth and Franklin streets. Also at this intersection is the Columbus Inn, a bed and breakfast establishment located in the former city hall.

Park along the street somewhere around the visitor's center. You can purchase a map of Columbus and Bartholomew County at the visitor's center and watch a slide show about Columbus architecture. Before your ride, visit the Irwin Gardens (open weekends during the day), which is just east of the starting location. This beautiful formal garden is maintained by a full-time gardener.

Columbus

Columbus, Indiana, is best known for its modern architecture, although there are a number of fine old buildings as well, including the visitor's center, the Bartholomew County Courthouse, and the old city hall. Many of the old storefronts in the downtown area have been restored and are quite attractive.

The era of modern architecture in Columbus began with the First Christian Church in 1942. Its most distinctive feature is the 166-foot bell tower, which can be seen from a distance. The Cummins Engine Company fueled the modern building boom by offering to pay architectural fees for new schools if they were designed by nationally known architects. The city agreed, and twelve schools have been constructed under this plan, which was later expanded to include other public buildings. Some corporate buildings have also been designed by top architects, such as the Indiana Bell Switching Center. The visitor's center gladly presents a slide show that tells the stories behind these structures. It also offers a bus tour of them. Some of the modern buildings are quite beautiful, while others are . . . not. All of them have the virtue of being unique and worth seeing on this basis alone.

Two buildings that combine beauty and functionality are the Irwin Union Bank and the Cummins Engine Corporate Office. The Irwin Bank

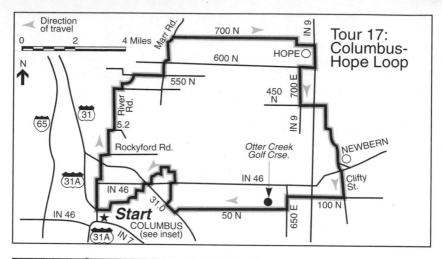

Tour 17: Columbus-Hope Loop

Direction of travel

0   2   4 Miles

N

65   31

Marr Rd.

700 N

600 N   HOPE

550 N

River Rd.

5.2

Rockyford Rd.

450 N   700 E

IN 9

NEWBERN

Otter Creek Golf Crse.

IN 46

Clifty St.

31A

IN 46

IN 46

Start
COLUMBUS (see inset)

50 N

650 E

100 N

31A   IN 7

31.0

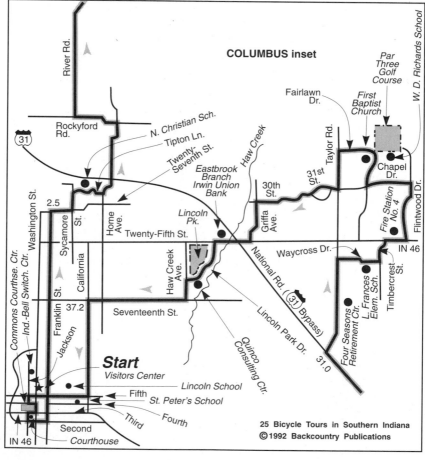

COLUMBUS inset

River Rd.

Rockyford Rd.

31

N. Christian Sch.

Tipton Ln.

Twenty-Seventh St.

Eastbrook Branch Irwin Union Bank

Haw Creek

Par Three Golf Course

Fairlawn Dr.

First Baptist Church

Taylor Rd.

W. D. Richards School

Chapel Dr.

Flintwood Dr.

Washington St.

2.5

Sycamore St.

Home Ave.

Lincoln Pk.

Twenty-Fifth St.

30th St.

31st St.

Griffa Ave.

Fire Station No. 4

IN 46

California

Franklin St.

37.2

Haw Creek Ave.

Seventeenth St.

National Rd. (31) Bypass

Waycross Dr.

Four Seasons Retirement Ctr.

L. Frances Elem. Sch.

Timbercrest St.

Commons Courthse. Ctr.

Ind.-Bell Switch. Ctr.

Jackson

Start
Visitors Center

Lincoln School

Fifth

St. Peter's School

Second   Third   Fourth

IN 46

Courthouse

Lincoln Park Dr.

Quinco Consulting Ctr.

31.0

25 Bicycle Tours in Southern Indiana
©1992 Backcountry Publications

provides a parklike setting for its drive-in customers and a well-lighted office for its employees. The Cummins building features an employee cafeteria that is glass on three sides and offers a pleasant view of a small pond and fountain. One building that turned out to be impractical is an elementary school designed by a California architect. His design featured multiple pagoda-type classrooms separated by patios. While this design might be fine for California, it was lousy for the cold winters and rainy springs of Indiana. The poor kids probably froze to death going from one room to another. The structure is now used as an adult education center.

The Quinco Consulting Center, one of the most unique designs, was constructed over a small creek. Equally distinctive is the Indiana Bell Switching Center. The outside is reflecting glass, screened by a trellis of greenery and a row of trees. The building features bright yellow, orange, red, and blue pipes that house its heating and air-conditioning units. These look like something a child might draw in a coloring book.

Jean Tinguely's sculpture *Chaos I* is truly a most bizarre work of art. Once you see it, you will understand its name. Some people say that modern art is junk, but this one is literally made from scrap metal. *Chaos I* is about thirty feet high and weighs nearly seven tons. It is constantly in motion: the entire structure pivots a quarter turn, its screws revolve, a small rail car goes back and forth on a short piece of track, and bowling-ball-size metal spheres race clickety-clack down a tube. One cannot appreciate this sculpture through a photograph. You have to see and hear it in person to enjoy it.

For more information, contact the Columbus Visitor's Center, 506 Fifth Street, Columbus, IN 47201 (812) 372-1954.

0.0   **START by heading west on Fifth Street.**
            The Irwin Union Bank (1973) is on the right.

0.2   **LEFT on Jackson Street.**
            The Columbus Post Office (1970) is on the right.

0.3   **LEFT on Fourth Street.**
            The Commons Courthouse Center (1973) is on the right.

0.3   **RIGHT on Washington.**

0.4   **RIGHT on Third Street.**
            The Bartholomew County Courthouse (1874) is on the left.

0.5   **LEFT on Jackson Street.**

0.5   **LEFT on Second Street.**
            The *Republic* newspaper plant (1971) is on the right; city hall (1981) is on the right.

0.6   **LEFT on Franklin Street.**

The Indiana Bell Switching Center (1978) is on the left, between Sixth and Seventh streets.

2.5   RIGHT on Twenty-Seventh Street.

2.6   LEFT on Sycamore Street.

2.8   RIGHT on Tipton Lane.
The North Christian Church (1964) is on the left. It is nicknamed "the oilcan" because of its shape.

3.0   LEFT on Home Avenue.

3.6   LEFT on Rockyford Road.

4.0   RIGHT on River Road.

5.2   LEFT to stay on River Road.

6.8   LEFT to stay on River Road.

7.4   RIGHT on 550N.

8.8   LEFT on Marr Road.

10.4   RIGHT on 700N.

15.9   RIGHT on IN 9.
This is the town of Hope. At the corner is the Yellow Trail Museum. If you are hungry, the Heritage House Restaurant is especially well known for the real mashed potatoes, freshly baked bread with honey butter, and pies!

Hope
The town of Hope was originally founded by Moravians, the first Protestants. They originated in fifteenth-century Bohemia (part of present-day Czechoslovakia), when John Hus spoke out for Church reform. The Church hierarchy tolerated this until Hus condemned the sale of indulgences (as Martin Luther did later). After this, the Church decided Hus was a heretic, and he was burned at the stake in 1415 (standard punishment for a heretic). His followers organized themselves into a separate church and called themselves the Brethren. They were nearly wiped out during the Thirty Years War (1618-48). By the early 1700s, only a few Moravians remained in Bohemia and nearby Moravia. At this time Count Zinzendorf offered refuge to any of the Moravians who would come to his estate in Saxony (now part of Germany). Zinzendorf believed in Christian unity and invited other religious dissenters to his estate as well. Missionary activity led to the formation of Nazareth and Bethlehem in Pennsylvania, and a settlement near Salem, North Carolina. When the farmland in North Carolina began to give out and small

farmers were unable to compete against slave labor, Martin Hauser decided to move to Hope and form a new settlement. He was given two hundred dollars to purchase land and start a new congregation.

Hauser began work on the settlement in 1830. It was initially named Goshen, but had to be renamed three years later to obtain a post office, since there was already a Goshen in northern Indiana. At the outset, he attempted to recreate an economic system that had been used by the Moravian Church until 1762. Under this system, land was sold only to Moravians, although others could rent land. It was the responsibility of the town fathers to recruit all the craftsmen that were required to make the town economically successful. Although he was eventually able to get most of the tradesmen he needed from the Moravian settlements in Pennsylvania and North Carolina, Hauser felt the authorities back east were discouraging people from moving west. In a letter to his superiors he wrote, "Why is there no one to come here? There are no murderers or cannibals. We live in a very nice friendly settlement." In 1836, money was needed to build a larger church. Despite objections by Hauser, it was decided to sell lots in Hope to raise money. This opened Hope up to non-Moravians and ended the church-controlled economic system.

Today Hope is a typical small Hoosier town of about two thousand. The Moravian church is still there, one of only three in Indiana today. John Henry Kluge, one of the first white children born in Indiana (1805), is buried in the graveyard by the church. The Yellow Trail Museum, located in a former hardware store, displays artifacts of the town's history. The museum's name came from a clever businessman's ad campaign. Elda Spaugh, owner of Spaugh's Garage, painted yellow bands on telephone poles. These yellow bands created routes that led to Hope like spokes on a wheel. Spaugh's Garage was then billed as "Home of the Yellow Trail."

The Moravian church and cemetery are on your right as you leave Hope. The Hope Elementary School is on your left.

16.8   **RIGHT on 600N.**

17.3   **LEFT on 700E.**

18.8   **LEFT on 450N.**

19.3   **CROSS IN 9.**
         Stay on 450N as it doglegs, and continue into the town of Newbern.

22.3   **RIGHT on Clifty Street.**

23.5   **RIGHT on 100N.**

24.8   **CROSS IN 9.**

Irwin Gardens

25.8   LEFT on 650E.

26.3   RIGHT on 50N.
On your right is the Otter Creek Golf Course, the top golf course in Indiana. It was designed by Robert Trent Jones, who said that its hole number 13 was the best he ever designed. Nicknamed Alcatraz, it is a 185-yard par three to an island green, framed by sycamore trees. The Clifty Creek Elementary School (1982) is on the left, just before US 31.

30.6   RIGHT on US 31.

31.0   RIGHT on Taylor Road.
The Four Seasons Retirement Center (1967) is on the right.

31.8   RIGHT on Waycross Drive.
L. Frances Elementary School (1969) is on the right.

32.1   LEFT on Timbercrest Street.

32.3   RIGHT on IN 46.
Fire Station No. 4 (16) is on the left.

32.5   LEFT on Flintwood Drive.

32.9   LEFT on Chapel Drive.

33.3   RIGHT on Fairlawn Drive.

The First Baptist Church (1965) is on your left; W. D. Richards Elementary School (1965) is on the right; then Par Three Golf Clubhouse (1972) is also on the right.

33.8   LEFT on Taylor Road.

34.2   RIGHT on 31st Street.

After winding around, this becomes 30th Street.

34.8   LEFT on Griffa Avenue.

35.2   RIGHT on 25th Street.

The Irwin Union Bank, Eastbrook Branch (1961) is on the right.

35.6   LEFT on Lincoln Park Drive.

Be alert! This road looks like a driveway going into a parking lot, so it's easy to miss. The Lincoln Center (1958) is on the right. Quinco Consulting Center (1972) is on the left.

36.3   LEFT on Hawcreek Avenue.

36.4   RIGHT on 17th Street.

37.2   LEFT on California Street.

38.0   RIGHT on Fifth Street.

The Lincoln Elementary School (1967) is on the right; St. Peter's Lutheran Church on the left. Then Cleo Rogers Memorial Library (1969) is on the right; First Christian Church (1942) is on the left. The Irwin Gardens is on the right just before you return to the visitor's center.

38.3   RETURN to the visitor's center.

After completing the tour, visit the commons and take a look at *Chaos I*. If you are thirsty, have an old-fashioned soda at Zaharako's Confectionery. Notice the onyx soda fountains. They were purchased from the St. Louis World Exposition in 1905. The German pipe organ there was purchased in 1908. They will be glad to play it for you if you ask them.

For more information, read "A Look at Architecture-Columbus, Indiana," published by the Visitor's Center in Columbus.

Bicycle Repair Services

Bicycle Station, 1005 25th, Columbus, IN 47201 (812) 379-9005.
Columbus Schwinn Cyclery, 833 16th, Columbus, IN 47201 (812) 372-7486.

18

Madison-Vevay Loop

48 miles; hilly to moderately rolling

This Ohio River tour features the town of Madison, once called the "New Orleans of the Midwest" because of its beautiful homes. The town's streets along the river contain examples of nearly every type of nineteenth-century architecture, including Gothic, Georgian, Regency, Classic Revival, Federal, and Americanized Italian Villa. Every trip to Madison reveals a new site or event to ponder and appreciate.

This tour also features Vevay, another historic river town with many beautiful old river homes; the birthplace of Edward and George Eggleston; and a most scenic, flat, and serene ride along the Ohio River.

Madison was called the "New Orleans of the Midwest" because of its beautiful homes and abundance of locally made wrought-iron fences and decorations. One hundred thirty-three blocks of Madison are in the National Registry of Historic Places. Surrounded by five-hundred-foot-high hills, Madison is nestled in the Ohio River valley. Its population is more than 13,000.

Madison is the county seat of Jefferson County, named in honor of Thomas Jefferson. It was laid out in 1810 by John Paul, Jonathon Lyons, and Lewis Davis. A county courthouse and log jail were built in 1811, and a newspaper, the *Western Eagle*, was published there two years later.

The town's golden years were from 1830 to 1855, when agricultural products were sent to Madison for shipping up and down the Ohio River. Work was plentiful in the town, and its population nearly doubled every decade. As the southern terminus of the Michigan Road and the Madison and Indianapolis Railroad, it was the starting point for many settlers moving north into the state.

The railroad's grade was so steep that the first engines lacked the power to climb out of the valley. In 1868 a massive engine, the *Reuben Wells*, was built expressly for the purpose of pulling railroad cars up the grade. The *Reuben Wells* was in service until 1905. It is presently on display at the Indianapolis Children's Museum.

Businessman and attorney James Lanier moved to Madison in 1817 and was instrumental in promoting the railroads and the town's local banking industry. In 1844 work was completed on his palatial mansion on the river at 500 West First Street. It is one of the finest examples of the

Classical Revival style in the state. Lanier moved to New York in 1849. All together, four generations of Laniers lived in the mansion. In 1925 the Lanier Mansion was given to the state and became its first memorial.

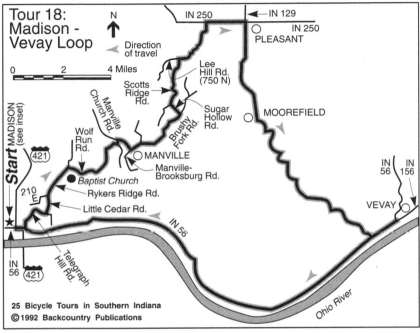

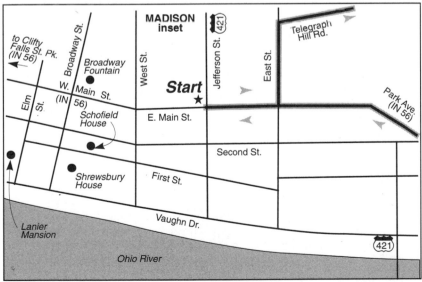

After the Civil War, Madison grew much more slowly, and with the arrival of the twentieth century, its population began to decline. Despite its sound local economy, Madison was surpassed by many other Hoosier cities in population and industrial growth.

Today, Madison hosts several festivals and events. At the Chautauqua of the Arts, held in late September, craftspeople from throughout the region display their wares in a street festival around the Lanier mansion. Walking tours of public and private homes are held in conjunction with the festival. For the Madison Regatta, held on July Fourth, a race course is laid out on the Ohio River, and the thunder of unlimited hydroplanes can be heard throughout the area.

Just outside Madison is Clifty Falls State Park, where electric and primitive camping is available and beautiful hiking trails are numerous. One of the most beautiful sights at the park is the autumn full moon rising over the hilltops and shining on the Ohio River. Numerous hotels and restaurants are available in Madison.

The list of Madison's historic buildings and homes is too long for a full description here, but some of the more prominent structures are listed below. Contact the Madison Area Chamber of Commerce, 301 East Main Street, Madison, IN 47250 for more information.

Some of the more notable buildings include:

- Judge Jeremiah Sullivan House, built in 1818, 304 West Second Street;
- Shrewsbury House, built in 1849, 301 West First Street;
- Talbott-Hyatt House and Garden, built in 1820s, 301 West Second Street;
- Madison Presbyterian Church, built in 1848, 202 Broadway;
- Broadway Fountain, built in 1876, Broadway Street;
- Francis Costigan House, built in 1849, 408 West Third Street;
- First Baptist Church, built in 1860, 416 Vine Street;
- Schofield House, built in 1817, 217 West Second Street.

0.0 **START at the intersection of US 421 and IN 56 (Main and Jefferson streets).**

0.0 **EAST on IN 56, or Main Street.**

0.1 **LEFT on East Street.**

0.3 **RIGHT on Telegraph Hill Road.**
Caution: This is a very steep grade.

1.9 **LEFT at an unmarked intersection onto Little Cedar Road.**
(This road is marked by a "no outlet" sign and goes back into a posh area now under development.) The road's name changes to Ryker's Ridge Road at the intersection of 210E. Continue on Ryker's Ridge Road. Its name changes again, at 250E, to Wolf Run Road. At the intersection at the Ryker's

Fountain in Madison

Ridge Baptist Church in Ryker's Ridge (no facilities) continue straight. Following this road, you enter a sprawling settlement called Manville.

5.7   ENTER Manville.

5.7   LEFT at the two-way stop in Manville.
         Cross over Indian-Kentuck Creek.

5.8   RIGHT on Manville Church Road.

6.7   LEFT on Manville-Brooksburg Road.
         (There is a convenience store at this intersection.)

7.5   RIGHT at the Y onto Brushy Fork Road.

8.6   LEFT onto Sugar Hollow Road.
         This intersection is unmarked. Immediately cross an old bridge over the Brushy Fork Creek.

10.7   RIGHT at the unmarked T-intersection onto Scotts Ridge Road. (The road to the left is gravel.)

12.2   RIGHT on Lee Hill Road (750N).

14.5   RIGHT on IN 250.

16.0   RIGHT on IN 129.
         Pass through the communities of Pleasant (no facilities) and

Moorefield (which has a convenience store).

28.2   LEFT on IN 56.

28.2   ENTER Vevay (which has groceries, restaurants, and a hotel).
Vevay (pronounced *vee-vee*) was settled by Swiss immigrants in 1802 and was originally called New Switzerland. The first settlers brought their winemaking skills to the new land and planted many vineyards. The community still has a wine festival every August to commemorate its early history. Jean and Daniel Dufour laid out the town in 1813 and changed its name to Vevay. After the Civil War, the winemaking industry declined and was replaced by furniture manufacturing. The town's economy is now based upon agricultural products and tobacco.

Most of the historic homes in Vevay are privately owned and are not open for tours. Like the Madison homes, they are too numerous to list in this text. A listing is available at the Switzerland County Historical Museum at East and Market streets, housed in an old Presbyterian church. The Switzerland County Courthouse is on Main Street and was built in 1864. Below the courthouse is a cellar that was used as a station on the Underground Railroad for escaping slaves.

The birthplace of Edward and George Eggleston, major Hoosier authors, is located at 306 West Main Street. Edward Eggleston is known for his 1817 book *The Hoosier Schoolmaster*. In 1900, he was elected president of the American Historical Association. George Eggleston fought in the Confederate Army and became the editor of the *New York Evening Post*.

28.9   TURN AROUND to head west on IN 56, and follow the river back to Madison (20 miles).
The gently rolling Ohio River is in view for much of this pedal. Because the road runs along the river, it is relatively flat and sheltered from the wind. Stop and savor the river's serenity. Watch for traffic!

48.2   RETURN to Madison.

Bicycle Repair Service
Madison Schwinn, 2034 Lanier Drive, Madison, IN 47250 (812) 273-4278.

19

The Laughery Valley: Weekender

88 miles; moderate with a few hills
Osgood to Rising Sun (40 miles), to Aurora (9 miles), back to Osgood (39 miles)

The main features of this weekender tour through Ripley, Deerborn and Ohio counties are scenery, river towns, homes, and early settlement history. It is here that George Rogers Clark suffered his only defeat. You'll pass the Tyson Temple, constructed of glazed ivory brick, glass, and aluminum, with a one-hundred-foot aluminum spire; Gordon's Leap; early stone walls; headquarters of the National Muzzle Loading Rifle Association; and a 1920s champion racing boat.

The Laughery Valley was settled very early in Indiana's history. Starting in Versailles State Park, Laughery creek winds through Ripley and Dearborn counties. Many of the earliest settlers built homes near this water source. At times the creek broadens and seems to be almost a river as it cuts through the rugged countryside. Evidence of the expanse of this creek in prehistoric times can be seen as you pedal along the edge of the valley outside Versailles. From IN 129, which runs along the rim, you can peer down into a vast valley dotted with small farms.

The Laughery Valley, just outside Aurora, was the scene of the only defeat that George Rogers Clark suffered during the Revolutionary War. In 1781, Colonel Archibald Lochery and 102 troops were bringing supplies to Clark's army, to be used in a campaign to attack Detroit. On August 24, as they were making camp at the mouth of Laughery Creek, the group was attacked by a large group of Indians. Only two men escaped; thirty-six were killed and sixty-four were taken to Detroit as prisoners. Lochery was tomahawked and scalped, along with the wounded men who were unable to make the march to Detroit. The loss of these troops and supplies prevented Clark from mounting his attack on Detroit. A marker at the mouth of the creek marks the site of the battle. An enactment of this battle was the last event of the recent national celebration of the Revolutionary War Bicentennial.

The tour begins in Osgood on US 421, at Jac-Cen-Del High School at the north edge of town. The school's unique name derives from the consolidation of three separate schools into one.

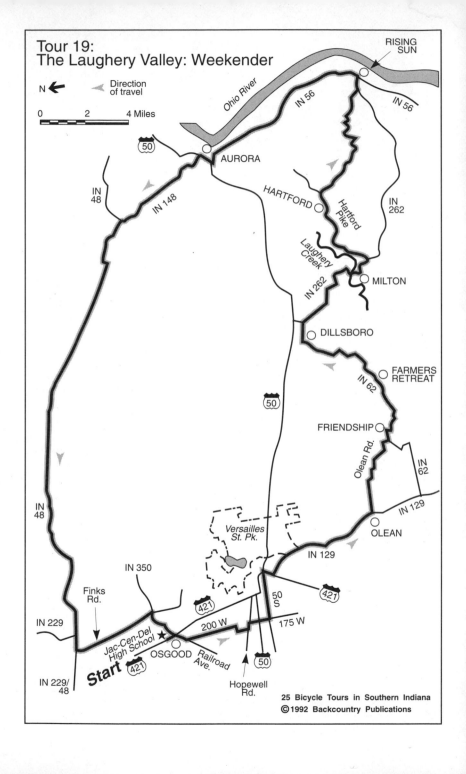

Tour 19:
The Laughery Valley: Weekender

N ← | Direction of travel

0   2   4 Miles

RISING SUN

Ohio River

IN 56

IN 56

50

AURORA

IN 48

IN 148

HARTFORD

Hartford Pike

IN 262

Laughery Creek

IN 262

MILTON

DILLSBORO

FARMERS RETREAT

IN 62

50

FRIENDSHIP

Olean Rd.

IN 62

IN 48

IN 129

Versailles St. Pk.

OLEAN

IN 129

IN 350

421

50 S

421

Finks Rd.

IN 229

200 W

175 W

Jac-Cen-Del High School

★

Start 421

OSGOOD

Railroad Ave.

50

IN 229/ 48

Hopewell Rd.

25 Bicycle Tours in Southern Indiana
©1992 Backcountry Publications

Osgood was platted in 1856 and incorporated in 1878. The town was named after A. L. Osgood, the chief engineer of the Ohio Mississippi Railroad in that area. Located in Osgood is the Damm Theater, a four-hundred-seat movie house. Interesting homes are abundant throughout the town. Take a few minutes to pedal the quiet streets before you embark on the tour.

0.0   START at the Jac-Cen-Del High School.

0.0   LEFT (South) on US 421.

0.7   RIGHT on Railroad Avenue.
Railroad Avenue is in the middle of Osgood and runs parallel to the railroad tracks.

1.0   LEFT on 350N, and cross the railroad tracks. LEFT onto 200W.

2.9   LEFT on Hopewell Road.

3.2   RIGHT on 175W.
Cross US 50/US 421.

4.0   LEFT on 50S.

5.7   RIGHT on US 421, and enter Versailles (where there are restaurants, groceries, a hotel, and camping). Stay on US 421 as it turns right at the stoplight.
Versailles (pronounced *ver-sales*) is the county seat of Ripley County. The courthouse was erected during the Civil War, and several additions have been added since that time. Versailles was platted in 1818 and named after Versailles, France. Confederate General John Morgan "visited" Versailles during his foray into Indiana.

James Tyson, cofounder of Walgreen drugstores, was a native of Versailles. He endowed the town with a school, church, library, and water works. The Tyson Temple, located at the corner of Tyson and Adams streets, is a very bizarre structure constructed from a variety of materials, including glazed ivory brick, glass brick, and aluminum. A one-hundred-foot cast-aluminum spire dominates the town. All angles on the structure have been rounded, including the roof. This building, with its composite of different architectural styles, seems almost to come out of science fiction.

In 1897, five prisoners were lynched in Versailles. Citizens shot or beat these men out of frustration over a wave of robberies and burglaries. The victims were then hung from a tree in the town. Every piece of the "hanging tree" was acquired for souvenirs. The state attorney general's office covered up the crime by stating in its records that the prisoners selected the ropes and hung themselves—believe it or not.

Just outside Versailles is Versailles State Park, where both primitive and electric camping are available. The park has a lake, a swimming beach, and beautiful hiking trails. Within the park is Gordon's Leap, whose name comes from a strange tale. Two medical students, Gordon and Glass, were caught trying to exhume a body at the local cemetery for dissection. Glass escaped, but Gordon was cornered at the edge of a hundred-foot cliff. To avoid capture, Gordon leaped from the cliff and survived, only breaking a leg. He dragged himself to a nearby cabin, where he obtained a horse and fled. Eventually, he enlisted in the Union Army and rose to the rank of major. After the Civil War he was nominated as the state's attorney general.

Leave the park and return to US 421 by retracing your path.

7.1   LEFT on IN 129.

12.6   LEFT on Olean Road, in the town of Olean.

Be careful—there is a steep, booming downhill. There are some excellent examples of early stone wall construction along this road. Built without mortar, these walls have survived nearly two hundred years and will no doubt survive many more.

16.0   LEFT on IN 62.

Pass through the towns of Friendship (which has a grocery), Farmers Retreat (with no facilities), and Dillsboro (which has a restaurant and grocery).

Friendship, established in 1849, was originally called Hart's Mill. The name was changed to Friendship in 1870 as a tribute to the area's residents. Friendship is also the headquarters for the National Muzzle Loading Rifle Association. Rendezvous where members gather to recreate the pioneer era are held throughout the year. Authentic costumes, weapons, and lodging dominate the community, and many events are held to show off the participants' skills and craftsmanship.

Dillsboro was established in 1830 and named for a prominent local citizen, James Dill.

24.5   RIGHT on IN 262 outside of Dillsboro.

You will pas through Milton on IN 262.

Milton was established in 1825 by James Pickney, who originally named it Jamestown. The name was changed to Guionsville in 1837 with the establishment of a post office. In 1850 the name was changed to Milton. At the edge of town along the route there is a Civil War-era cemetery that has beautiful headstones.

29.0   LEFT on Hartford Pike.

This road comes right after you cross a concrete bridge over Laughery Creek, about .75 miles after Milton.

33.0   ENTER the town of Hartford.
Hartford was established in 1817 and is apparently named for a town in England.

33.3   RIGHT on Nelson Road, at the first intersection after leaving Hartford.

39.5   ENTER Rising Sun.
Rising Sun is the county seat of Ohio County, Indiana's smallest county. It was founded in 1814 by John James. Its name is supposed to derive from the beauty of an Ohio River sunrise. The courthouse was built in 1845 and still serves the county. The Ohio County Historical Society Museum has some interesting artifacts, including the *Hoosier Boy*, a famous racing boat of the 1920s, a quilt collection, and a variety of coin-operated musical devices. The Rising Sun Seminary, located on Fourth Street, claims to be the state's oldest normal school. Established in 1827, the school changed its name to the Indiana Teachers Seminary in 1836. Many of the grand old homes along the river, on Front Street, were destroyed in a massive flood in 1937. Row houses, built in the 1820s, survived the flood, evidence of the quality of many of the town's structures.

Facilities here include restaurants, camping, and a bed and breakfast.

39.6   LEFT on IN 262 (Main Street) in Rising Sun.

40.0   LEFT on IN 56 and follow it into Aurora. IN 56 winds through Aurora- be sure to follow the signs.

48.1   ENTER Aurora.
Aurora, established in 1819, serves as the hub of the area's agribusiness. Formerly a busy river town, its golden era passed with the passing of the steamboat. Many interesting buildings and homes can be found throughout the town. The most interesting is the Hillforest Mansion, located on Fifth Street. Built by Thomas Gaff in 1856, the mansion's most distinctive feature is its cupola in the shape of a steamboat's pilot house. The cupola offers an expansive view of the Ohio River.

48.2   RIGHT on US 50.

48.7   LEFT on IN 148.

53.5   LEFT on IN 48.
There are several groceries and an orchard along this road, but no restaurants. This is nice stretch (30 miles) of secondary highway with little traffic.

View from the porch of the Hillforest Manor in Aurora

83.1   CONTINUE STRAIGHT on IN 229 at the intersection of IN 48 and IN 229.

83.6   LEFT on Finks Road.

86.9   RIGHT on IN 350. Follow it back into Osgood.

88.6   RIGHT on US 421.

88.7   RETURN to Jac-Cen-Del High School.

Bicycle Repair Service
Thomas Bike & Frame Shop, 127 Eads Parkway, Lawrenceburg, IN 47025 (812) 537-4433.

20

The Michigan Road, Route 1

Shelbyville-Greensburg
45 miles; easy

The Michigan Road, the highlight of this tour, was the first road through Indiana. It connected the Ohio River with Lake Michigan. The tour also features a large-tooth aspen tree growing out of the courthouse tower in Greensburg.

The Michigan Road
Prior to statehood in 1816, Indiana's roads consisted of Indian trails, animal trails (like the Buffalo Trace), and military expedition roads.

Even after the relocation of the state capital to Indianapolis in 1825, the northern half of the state was legally owned by Native Americans. Leaders recognized that the only way the state would see any growth was by improving its internal transportation system.

The Enabling Act of 1816, which brought Indiana into statehood, allowed the state to receive three percent of the proceeds from the sale of public lands to be applied toward transportation. Through a series of "treaties" in the 1820s, the Native Americans surrendered their title to these lands, and many of them were moved west of the Mississippi River.

The first project in this push for internal improvements was the building of a road that would connect the Ohio River with Lake Michigan. It was started in 1826 and finished in 1837. The exact route of this first road, called the Michigan Road, was much debated. The final route started in Madison, on the Ohio River, went northwest through Versailles, Greensburg, and Shelbyville to the new state capital, Indianapolis. From Indianapolis, the road went directly north to South Bend, then curved northwest again to its terminus in Michigan City. Eventually, more than 170,000 acres of land were surveyed and dedicated to the building of the Michigan Road.

To call the early Michigan Road a road is a real stretch of the imagination. After the land was surveyed, trees were cut only to the point that their stumps could be cleared by a wagon passing over them. No surface was laid over the road. Consequently, a trip up the road consisted of a jolting ride over a rough, often muddy, path that tested man, animal, and wagon. One early jokester described the road as being variously dry, navigable, or impossible. Eventually, the road was cleared and surfaced. It served as a vital artery in opening the northern half of the state to early settlement.

The coming of the railroad in the 1850s diminished the importance of the Michigan Road. US 421 now connects these Michigan Road towns, but since US 421 often does not use the original route, much of the original Michigan Road is now relegated to county roads. Today you can pedal through the countryside encountering only light traffic. Houses on the route testify to the area's age and history. You will see beautiful homes and massive churches that seem out of place on a lonely county road. Enjoy the pedal, and revel in an area that was so much a part of the state's early history.

The tour starts at the J. C. Penney shopping center, located at the I-74/IN 44 exit at the south edge of Shelbyville (which has a restaurant, grocery, hotel, and camping). There is plenty of parking in the shopping center's parking lot.

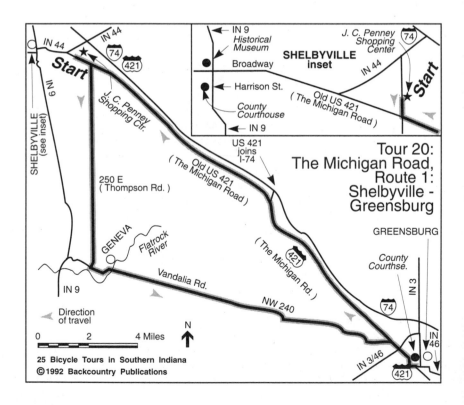

Shelbyville

Shelbyville, the county seat of Shelby County, has about 15,000 residents. Platted in 1822, it housed as many as nineteen furniture factories at the start of the twentieth century. The Great Depression doomed the town's industry. Presently, the city hosts a variety of industries and is a bedroom community for Indianapolis.

The Shelby County Courthouse is a steel and concrete structure surfaced with Indiana limestone. It was built in 1936 with the assistance of a WPA grant from the Roosevelt administration.

Charles Major, author of *The Bears of Blue River* and *When Knighthood Was in Flower*, was from Shelbyville. Grover Cleveland's vice president, Thomas Hendricks, also hailed from Shelbyville. Hendricks died less than a year after being inaugurated.

An historical marker on IN 7 notes that Shelbyville was the site of the state's first railroad in 1834. Shelbyville has two major festivals, the Blue River Valley Craft Fair in early October, and the Bears of Blue River Festival in late August-early September. The Shelby County Historical Museum, located at 52 West Broadway, is open on Saturdays and Sundays.

0.0   START in the J. C. Penney shopping center, located at the I-74/IN 44 exit at the southeast edge of Shelbyville

(where there is a restaurant, grocery, hotel, and camping).

0.0   LEFT on Progress Road.

0.3   LEFT on OLD US 421 (Michigan Road).

1.5   RIGHT on 250E (also known as Thompson Road).

9.8   LEFT on Vandalla Road.

This is a great little road that follows the Flatrock River for a while. Take your time and enjoy the scenery. Jog right at a set of trash dumpsters, cross the Flatrock River, and enter the town of Geneva (which has a convenience store). Vandalia Road becomes NW240 when you cross into Decatur County (about five miles past Geneva). Geneva was originally called Sulphur Hill. It was platted in 1853.

22.8   RIGHT on US 421, and follow it into Greensburg. Be careful-the traffic can be heavy.

22.8   ENTER Greensburg.

Greensburg, the county seat of Decatur County, was founded in 1821 and incorporated in 1837. It serves the mixed economies of the county, industry, and farming. It was named after Revolutionary War hero Major General Nathanael Greene. Over two-thirds of the land in the county is used for agribusiness. The Decatur County Courthouse was built in 1860 and is an exceptional example of Gothic architecture.

Touring Bikes on Vandalia Road

Greensburg's most unique feature is a large-tooth aspen tree that grows from the spire of the county courthouse. It was first discovered growing there more than eighty years ago. Its origin and how it maintains its nutrients for continued growth remain a mystery. The town proudly proclaims the tree in brochures and billboards throughout the area.

The Decatur County Historical Society Museum is located in the Knights of Pythias Building and Theater, at 215 North Broadway. Built in 1899, the theater was one of the first in the region to show talking pictures; it even had air conditioning. Greensburg claims several famous people as natives or residents, including Carl Fisher (cofounder of the Indianapolis Motor Speedway) and race-car driver Wilbur Shaw.

25.4   NORTH (turn around) out of Greensburg following US 421, the Michigan Road.

Just before the junction of US 421 and I-74, turn LEFT onto Michigan Road and follow it through the countryside back to Shelbyville (20 miles).

44.7   RIGHT on Progress Road.

45.0   RETURN to the shopping center.

21

The Michigan Road, Route 2

Greensburg - Versailles
61 miles; easy and flat

This tour includes the large-tooth aspen growing from the spire of the county courthouse in Greensburg; an early talking picture theater; the Tyson Temple; the scene of a lynching; and of course the Michigan Road. See The Michigan Road, Route 1 (Tour 20) for more details.

This tour starts in Greensburg, in Decatur County. A variety of convenient places are available there for parking. You can even park your car on the town square, which gives you a good opportunity to see the town.

0.0   START at the Decatur County Courthouse in Greensburg. Head south on US 421 out of Greensburg.

0.8   RIGHT on 60E, which is also called Millhousen Road.

8.6   LEFT on 820S (marked by a sign for the town of Millhousen).
You are still on Millhousen Road. The road winds through the town of Millhousen after the turn (the town has a restaurant and grocery).

10.6   ENTER Millhousen.
Millhousen was settled in the 1830s by German Catholics. It was named after the German hometown of the settlers' leader, Maximilian Schneider. Religion has always been a focal point of the area-the first parish was established in the early 1840s. St. Mary's Catholic Church is a prominent landmark in the countryside. Built in 1860, its 175-foot steeple dominates the landscape. Take a little time, pedal through the town, and examine the construction of the homes and use of locally made brick.

10.7 Be careful-there is a steep, narrow downhill across a small bridge just after you leave Millhousen. Follow Millhousen Road (800S) through the countryside to the town of Napoleon.

16.4   RIGHT on US 421, and pedal through Napoleon (which has a restaurant and grocery).
Napoleon, named after Napoleon Bonaparte, was established in 1820.

16.7 **RIGHT on 850N, which is at the southern edge of Napoleon. Be careful-don't pass it.**

16.9 **LEFT on Old Michigan Road, and follow it through the countryside.**

24.4 **LEFT on Hopewell Road at the community of Dabney.**

27.7 **RIGHT on 175W. Cross US 50.**

28.5 **LEFT on 50S.**

Tour 21:
The Michigan Road,
Route 2:
Greensburg - Versailles

N

Direction of travel

0   2   4 Miles

25 Bicycle Tours in Southern Indiana
©1992 Backcountry Publications

Pumpkin festival parade in Versailles

30.2   RIGHT on US 421/US 50.

31.6   ENTER Versailles. Caution: heavy traffic.

Versailles (*ver sales*) is the county seat of Ripley County. The county courthouse was erected during the Civil War. Be sure to visit the Tyson Tomple (see Tour 19) while you are here.

In 1897 Versailles was the scene of the lynching of five prisoners (see Tour 19 for details). Don't miss Versailles State Park, where electric and primitive camping are both available, as well as a lake, swimming beach, and beautiful hiking trails. Gordon's Leap, the site of a daring escape, is also here (see Tour 19).

In late September, the Pumpkin Festival is held in Versailles. It is the major event of the area, complete with a parade and festival queen.

31.6   HEAD North (TURN AROUND) out of Versailles on US 421/US 50.

33.0   LEFT on 50S.

34.7   RIGHT on 175W. Cross US 50.

35.5   LEFT on Hopewell Road.

35.8   RIGHT on 200W. The road will curve and become 350N outside of Osgood.

38.7 **RIGHT on Railroad Avenue in Osgood**
just after crossing some railroad tracks. This road parallels the tracks.

39.0 **LEFT on US 421.**
Be careful-traffic can be heavy.

44.8 **LEFT on Millhousen Road at Napoleon. Follow it through Millhousen.**

52.6 **RIGHT on 60E (still Millhousen Road), and follow it back to Greensburg.**

60.5 **LEFT on US 421.**

61.3 **RETURN to the courthouse.**

22

Oldenburg

53 miles; moderately hilly; the last 15 miles are especially hilly

"The Village of Spires," Oldenburg, is where this Franklin County tour begins. It visits Metamora, a shoppers' paradise that also offers a slice of the canal history of Indiana; and Brookville, the political and cultural center of early Indiana.

If you would like to split the ride into two days, camping is available at Whitewater Memorial State Park or Mounds State Recreation Area. There are several bed and breakfast establishments in Metamora and a motel in Brookville. Take your time on this ride—there are a lot of sights to see.

Oldenburg is three miles north of Batesville on IN 229, which someone once told me is "the crookedest road in the world." Batesville is halfway between Indianapolis and Cincinnati along Interstate 74.

Before starting your ride, take some time to observe the beautiful architecture in Oldenburg. In addition to its three major spires, there are many charming old buildings. Eighty of the 115 buildings in the historic district were built before 1900. If you like old buildings, this is your kind of town.

Oldenburg was platted in 1837 by two German Catholics and named for their hometown in northern Germany. They wanted it to be a German Catholic town, so when they recruited new settlers, they went to Cincinnati and passed out handbills that were printed in German. Eventually a church, convent, and monastery were established. Unfortunately, the archbishop decided to destroy the monastery in 1986, despite local efforts to preserve it. For information about convent tours, call (812) 934-2475.

The Oldenburg Preservation Association has produced a small brochure that describes fifty (forty-nine now that the monastery was wiped out) of the town's buildings that can be viewed on a short walking tour. Keep in mind that all the buildings are privately owned. Tours of the convent's main buildings can be arranged by appointment only. During the town's July festival, "Freudenfest," tours are given by local historians. Oldenburg's architecture is particularly rich because of Casper Gaupel, a master tinsmith who did the pressed metal ornamentation on some of the buildings. Some of the interesting restaurants in

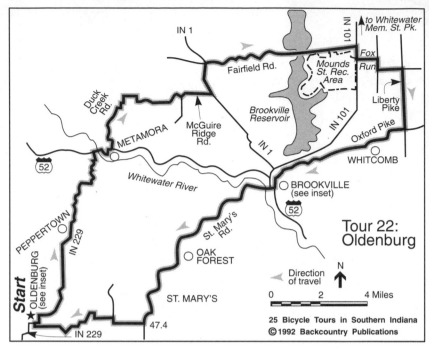

IN 1

→ to Whitewater Mem. St. Pk.

IN 101

Fox Run

Fairfield Rd.

Mounds St. Rec. Area

Liberty Pike

Duck Creek Rd.

Brookville Reservoir

Oxford Pike

McGuire Ridge Rd.

METAMORA

IN 1

IN 101

WHITCOMB

52

Whitewater River

BROOKVILLE (see inset)

52

PEPPERTOWN

IN 229

St. Mary's Rd.

Tour 22: Oldenburg

OAK FOREST

N

Start

OLDENBURG (see inset)

ST. MARY'S

Direction of travel

0   2   4 Miles

25 Bicycle Tours in Southern Indiana
©1992 Backcountry Publications

47.4

IN 229

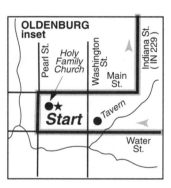

OLDENBURG inset

Pearl St.

Holy Family Church

Washington St.

Main St.

Indiana St. (IN 229)

Start

Tavern

Water St.

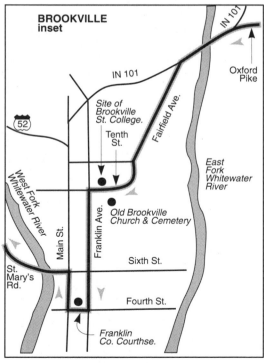

BROOKVILLE inset

IN 101

IN 101

Oxford Pike

IN 101

Fairfield Ave.

52

Site of Brookville St. College.

Tenth St.

East Fork Whitewater River

West Fork Whitewater River

Old Brookville Church & Cemetery

Main St.

Franklin Ave.

Sixth St.

St. Mary's Rd.

Fourth St.

Franklin Co. Courthse.

town include Koch's Brau Haus, King's Tavern, and the Wagner Tavern.

0.0   **START the tour in the parking lot of the Holy Family Church on Main Street (IN 229).**

0.0   **RIGHT (East) on Main Street.**
Follow the twists and turns of IN 229. Pass through Peppertown, which is just a wide spot in the road, and proceed toward US 52. The terrain is gently rolling until you reach a steep and twisting downhill. A traffic sign warns truck drivers to shift into a lower gear, but this won't help much on a bicycle. Use caution going down this hill, especially if the road is wet, and stay on the righthand side at all times.

9.5   **RIGHT on US 52.**

9.6   **CROSS the Whitewater River.**

9.7   **RIGHT at the first road into Old Metamora.**

Metamora

This 1838 canal town was named after an Indian princess in a popular play of the time. It was a stop on the Whitewater Canal, which extended from Hagerstown to Cincinnati. Many Union soldiers went off to the Civil War by way of this canal, but they returned in 1865 by a railroad that had been laid on the canal's towpath. Eventually the "iron horse" put the Wabash and Erie Canal out of business as well. The State of Indiana reconstructed a fourteen-mile section of the canal from Laurel to Brookville, and Metamora is now filled with craft, antique, and other shops.

There are several interesting sights in Metamora. The state operates a gristmill that is powered by water from the canal. Periodically they demonstrate how corn was ground and then separated into cornmeal and other products. Cornmeal is sold at the mill, and at the Duck Creek Palace cornbread is made from corn ground at the mill (with no preservatives added). In the old days, flour from the mill was sold in the Whitewater Valley under the name Pride of The Valley.

At the east end of town is the Duck Creek Aqueduct. This impressive wooden structure carries the canal over Duck Creek. When it was restored, the original arches, a hundred years old, were used since no suitable replacements could be found. The *Ben Franklin*, a reproduction of a boat that once traveled up and down the canal, takes passengers through the aqueduct. The half-hour ride goes to the restored locks east of town and back. (To get a better look at the locks, which are capable of raising and lowering a boat, travel east of town on US 52 a short distance.)

While two horses pull the boat, a taped message tells some of

The Ben Franklin III

the colorful history of the canal. Years ago, when two boats came to a lock at the same time, the issue of who would lock through first was decided in a simple manner. They had a fight, and the winner went first. Sometimes only the captains fought, while other times the cooks and steersmen joined in as well. (Keep in mind that gentlemen of this time period settled their differences by dueling.)

Several historic buildings are located in Metamora. One of the most interesting is known as the Gingerbread House because of its trim. The builder was a carpenter for the railroad, and he used the ornamentation from several different railroad depots on this house. Another unique feature of this house is that it is built on seven different levels. For more information, contact: Metamora Historical Society, P.O. Box 97, Metamora, IN 47030. For canal history, look for: *Indiana Canals* by Paul Fatout (216 pages); *Metamora Canal Town* by Milford Anness (20 pages); and *Low Bridge and Locks Ahead* by Milford

Good restaurants in town include the Duck Creek Palace and the Hearthstone. The Hearthstone has the best food in the area, but it is located just east of town on US 52 instead of in Old Metamora itself. You might want to stop in here when you go down to see the locks. You may also be interested in the area's annual festivals: May Day (the first weekend in May); the Firemen's Festival (July); Canal Days (October); and Christmas Walk (December).

After visiting the town, return to US 52 by the same road.

10.9 **RIGHT on US 52.**

11.3 **LEFT (first left) onto Duck Creek Road.**

16.3 **LEFT at the T onto McGuire Ridge Road.**

17.7 **LEFT on IN 1.**
Caution: Traffic may be heavy, especially during the boating season.

19.1 **RIGHT on Fairfield Road.**

25.3 **RIGHT on IN 101.**

> 25.8 On the right is Mounds State Recreation Area. Camping is available here.

25.8 **LEFT on Fox Run (first left).**

26.8 **RIGHT at the T.**

27.3 **LEFT at the T.**

28.3 **RIGHT on Liberty Pike.**

31.0 **RIGHT on Oxford Pike (which is unmarked; there is a stop sign, and it's the second intersection).**
This road goes through Whitcomb (at 32.5) and into Brookville. Brookville is a good place to get something to eat and rest a bit before starting the hilliest portion of the ride.

Motel
Mound Haven Motel (on US 52) (317) 647-4149.

Restaurant:
Hertel's Cafeteria (370 Main Street).

Camping
Whitewater Memorial State Park, Route 2, Liberty IN 47353 (317) 458-5565; Brookville Reservoir, Route 1, Box 373C, Brookville, IN 47201 (317) 647-6557.

32.5 **ENTER Whitcomb.**

36.1 **LEFT on IN 101.**
Caution: There is a steep downhill when you come to a stop sign.

36.4 **LEFT on Fairfield Avenue.**

Brookville
With the Greeneville Treaty of 1795, the Indians allowed white settlement on land east of a line that passed two miles west of the present site of Brookville. Two Moravian missionaries arrived at the junction of the forks of the Whitewater River in 1801, although the town was not officially founded until 1808. Many settlers arrived in

the early 1800s by traveling up the Whitewater River. Brookville was
an early political center, and three governors (James Brown Ray,
Noah Noble, and David Wallace) lived there. David Wallace was
also the father of Lew Wallace, the Civil War general and author of
Ben-Hur.

Today Brookville is a small town of about 3,000 and is the
county seat of Franklin County. Folks from large cities will be
shocked to find parking meters that will accept pennies. A dam was
built north of Brookville in 1965 to provide flood control in the
Whitewater valley. The dam created Brookville Reservoir, which
also provides recreational boating and fishing. Camping is available at three locations along the reservoir.

For more information: Brookville Chamber of Commerce, Box
211, Brookville,IN 47012 (317) 647-3177.

37.0   BEAR RIGHT on Tenth Street.

37.0   On the left is the Old Brookville Church (built in 1820) and
cemetery.
On the right is the site of Brookville College (built in 1852).

37.1   LEFT on Franklin Avenue.

37.5   RIGHT on Fourth Street.

37.6   RIGHT on Main Street.
The Franklin County Courthouse is on the northeast corner, and
Hertel's Cafeteria is on the southwest corner.

**37.7   LEFT on Sixth Street, which crosses the Whitewater River and
becomes St. Mary's Road.**

43.6   ENTER the town of Oak Forest.
(there's a general store here).

46.8   ENTER the town of St. Mary's.
(there's a pop machine at the garage).

47.4   RIGHT to stay on St. Mary's Road.

52.9   RETURN to Oldenburg.
Two interesting buildings are at the corner of Water and Washington
streets. The building on the northeast corner was used as a tavern.
According to legend, some of Morgan's Raiders, Confederate
calvarymen led by John Hunt Morgan, drank beer here while their
horses were shod.

On the house at the northwest corner, note the unsupported
second-story balcony. The lower porch was removed to make way
for the sidewalk.

53.0   RIGHT on Pearl Street.

53.1   RIGHT on Main Street.

53.2   RETURN to the parking lot.

Proceed immediately to Koch's Brau Haus and order their famous fried chicken. You may want to order your favorite German beverage as well.

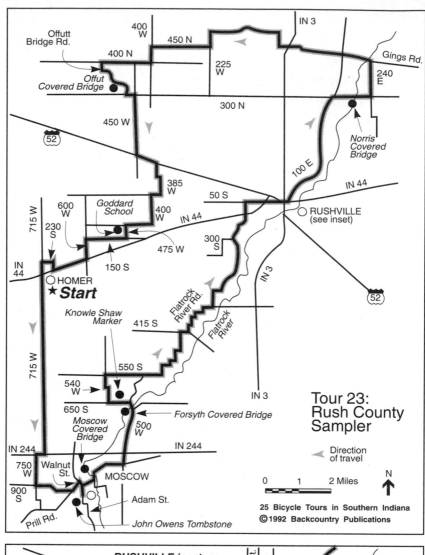

Offutt
Bridge Rd.

400 N

400 W

450 N

IN 3

Gings Rd.

Offut
Covered Bridge

225 W

240 E

300 N

Norris
Covered
Bridge

52

450 W

100 E

IN 44

385 W

50 S

Goddard
School

400 W

IN 44

RUSHVILLE
(see inset)

715 W

600 W

230 S

475 W

300 S

150 S

IN 44

HOMER

52

★ Start

IN 3

Knowle Shaw
Marker

415 S

Flatrock River Rd.

Flatrock River

715 W

550 S

540 W

650 S

IN 3

Moscow
Covered
Bridge

500 W

Forsyth Covered Bridge

Tour 23:
Rush County
Sampler

IN 244

IN 244

750 W

Walnut
St.

MOSCOW

Direction
of travel

900 S

Adam St.

0   1   2 Miles

N

Prill Rd.

John Owens Tombstone

25 Bicycle Tours in Southern Indiana
©1992 Backcountry Publications

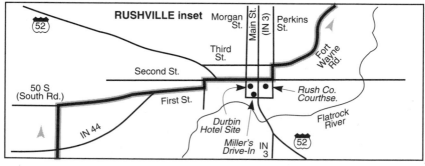

52

RUSHVILLE inset

Morgan
St.

Main St.
(IN 3)

Perkins
St.

Third
St.

Fort
Wayne
Rd.

Second St.

50 S
(South Rd.)

First St.

Rush Co.
Courthse.

IN 44

Durbin
Hotel Site

Miller's
Drive-In

IN 3

Flatrock
River

52

23

Rush County Sampler

50 miles; easy and flat

Highlights of this tour include the Sampler, a furniture manufacturer; four covered bridges; a one-room schoolhouse; Moscow; Wendell Wilkie's campaign headquarters; and the church of the preacher who wrote "Bringing in the Sheaves."

Rush County has numerous covered bridges because three generations of the Kennedy family, located in Rushville, constructed them. The local historical society has a model of a covered bridge that was used to demonstrate the sturdiness of their design. The model was placed between two chairs, and the salesman would stand on top of it.

Before you start your tour, you may wish to see a slide show about making furniture, courtesy of the Sampler. The only place for food and drink on this tour is in Rushville, which is about halfway through the route. This is a flat, easy route.

Start your tour in the Sampler parking lot in downtown Homer (8 miles west of Rushville on IN 44).

The Sampler

The town of Homer grew up around a sawmill. Since the mill produced many crossties for railroads, the town was nicknamed "Slabtown." One of the few businesses remaining in the town is the Sampler, which produces fine cherry furniture. The shop is located in a former tomato canning factory. The company has been operating since April 1, 1946. As they explain, "Everyone told us we were fools to locate in Homer, so we started on April Fool's Day." Feel free to stop by and say hello if you happen to pass through. The Sampler is open daily and Sunday afternoons. If you need any other information for your tour or would like to obtain the store's catalog, call or write: The Sampler, P.O. Box 68, Homer, IN 46146 (317) 663-2235.

0.0	**LEFT (south) on 715W.**
0.1	**RIGHT on IN 44.**
0.2	**LEFT on 725W after crossing bridge.**
5.6	**RIGHT on IN 244.**

Forsyth covered bridge

5.9   LEFT on 750W.

6.9   LEFT at 900S.

8.0   LEFT at the T, onto Prill Road.
Follow this road into Moscow, which was named for the Russian capital. There are a number of Amish folks in this area. Rumor has it there is an Amish bakery in the neighborhood, but its location changes every few weeks to stay ahead of the state health inspectors. The Amish don't use electricity, so their homes have no electric lines or TV antennas.

8.3   RIGHT on Walnut Street.

8.4   RIGHT on Adam Street.
Take this road past the church.

8.4   RIGHT into the cemetery.

8.6   The tombstone of John Owens can be found toward the center of the cemetery. It is a full-size replica of him crafted out of Italian marble. After it was completed, his family didn't think his bare head looked quite right during the cold winters, so a fedora was added. It became a popular prank to steal the fedora, although it would eventually reappear. To stop these pranks, the fedora was glued on. Unfortunately, it was destroyed when someone tried to pry it off.

8.6   **After leaving the cemetery, turn back toward Moscow.**

8.8   **LEFT at the T, onto Water Street.**

8.8   **RIGHT immediately, to cross the Moscow covered bridge, built in 1886.**

It is the only twin Burr arch bridge still in existence. It spans the Flatrock River, which is named for its large flat rocks. These rocks make excellent picnic spots.

8.9   **LEFT at the T, after the bridge.**

10.1   **LEFT at 500W.**

This road may get somewhat rough along the low spots near the river.

12.0   **LEFT at the T, onto 650S.**

12.0   This is the Forsyth covered bridge, built in 1888.

12.2   **LEFT at the Y.**

12.4   On the rock under the tree in front of the Flatrock Christian Church there is a historical marker in honor of Knowle Shaw (1834-1878). He preached at this church and wrote hundreds of hymns. His best-known work is "Bringing in the Sheaves." Shaw became very successful on the revival circuit and converted more than twenty thousand souls. He was killed in a train wreck in Texas.

12.9   **RIGHT at 540W.**

13.8   **RIGHT at 550S.**

17.4   **RIGHT at the T onto 415S.**

17.6   **LEFT at Flatrock River Road.**

18.9   **LEFT onto Flatrock River Road (again!).**

19.4   **RIGHT at the T onto 300S.**

22.2   **CROSS in 44.**

22.5   **RIGHT at the T onto 50S.**

23.2   **LEFT at the T onto IN 44.**

As it comes in on the right and its name changes to First Street. You are entering Rushville.

23.4   **LEFT at Pearl Street.**

23.5   **RIGHT at the T onto Second Street.**

23.7   The apartments at the southeast corner of Second and Morgan streets were once the Durbin Hotel. In 1940, this was the campaign headquarters for Wendell Wilkie, who was the Republican presidential candidate running against Franklin Roosevelt.

23.8   Miller's Drive-in, a popular local eating spot, is 0.2 miles south (turn right onto Main Street) off this route. The drive-in also has a small dining room with a wide variety of menu items.

23.9   There is a historical marker for Dr. Laughlin, who founded Rushville. He named it for Dr. Benjamin Rush, who was appointed Surgeon General of Armies of the Middle Department during the American Revolution. There is a historical marker on the north side of the Rush County Courthouse for Wendell Wilkie, the only native Hoosier to be nominated for president by a major party.

Wendell Wilkie
Wendell Wilkie was born in Elwood, but his wife (Edith Wilk) was born in Rushville. Originally a Democrat, Wilkie later became a Republican. In 1940 he became the surprise nominee for president after trailing far behind Thomas Dewey and Robert A. Taft on the first ballot. He established his campaign headquarters at the former Durbin Hotel in Rushville. After being defeated by Roosevelt, Wilkie wrote *One World*. He died in 1944 and was buried in East Hill Cemetery, about a half-mile east of Rushville on IN 44.

24.0   LEFT at the first intersection past the courthouse.

24.1   RIGHT at next intersection onto Third Street.
Follow this street as it curves north and becomes Fort Wayne Road, then 100E.

27.7   RIGHT on 300N.

28.2   Norris Covered Bridge, built in 1916.

28.7   LEFT on 240E.

29.9   LEFT at T onto Gings Road.

32.3   CROSS IN 3.

35.2   LEFT on 225W.

35.7   RIGHT onto 450N.

37.5   LEFT at the T onto 400W.

38.0   RIGHT on 400N.

39.5   LEFT on Offutt Bridge Road.

40.3   Offutt's Covered Bridge, built in 1884.

40.9   LEFT at the T onto 300N.

41.1   RIGHT on 450W.

42.9   LEFT at the T onto US 52.

43.7   RIGHT on 385W.

45.0   LEFT on 400W.

46.7   LEFT on 475W.

> 47.1 This is the Goddard School, a restored one-room school-house. Notice the water pump out front, and the two outhouses behind the school.

47.2   RIGHT at the T onto 150S.

48.4   LEFT at the T onto 600W.

49.0   RIGHT on IN 44.

49.4   RIGHT on 230S.

> 50.0 The large building on the left is a former tomato canning factory that is now used to produce cherry furniture by the Sampler.

50.2   RETURN to the Sampler parking lot.

24

James Whitcomb Riley Loop

28.6 miles; flat to gently rolling

The highlights of this tour include the family home of poet James Whitcomb Riley; the home of the rooster (the original) symbol of the Democratic Party; an interesting carving above the door of a library; and Knightstown, a community exceptional in the quality and quantity of preserved and restored homes.

James Whitcomb Riley is known as the Hoosier Poet. His poems include "The Ole Swimmin' Hole" and "Little Orphant Annie." Born in 1849 as the third of six children, he was named for James Whitcomb, an Indiana governor and senator. Riley's family had arrived in Greenfield five years earlier. Reuben Riley, his father, was a successful attorney and was elected to the state legislature at the age of twenty-six.

James scorned the confines of traditional education and became a multi-talented performer and musician. He was an actor, lecturer, and stage performer, and he traveled throughout the region. His poetry rang of the rural Hoosier dialect, which made his poetry internationally identifiable.

Riley eventually moved to Indianapolis, where he died in 1916. Indianapolis and Greenfield had a serious dispute over where Riley's remains would be interred. Eventually, Indianapolis prevailed, and he is buried at Crown Hill Cemetery.

The tour beings at the Hancock County Courthouse in Greenfield (which has convenience stores, grocery stores, restaurants, hotels/motels, and camping). There is ample parking at and near the courthouse.

Greenfield, the county seat of Hancock County, is a bedroom community to Indianapolis. It was platted as the county seat in 1828 along the route of the National Road. Greenfield is thought to be named for an early settler, John Green. The city is best known for its native son, James Whitcomb Riley. His childhood home, at 250 West Main Street, has been restored by the Riley Old Home Society and is open for tours. Next to the home is the home of John F. Mitchell, Jr. Mitchell's family founded the *Hancock Democrat* newspaper and later printed many of Riley's works. Minnie Belle Mitchell, John's mother, wrote several books about Riley. The Mitchell home is now called the Riley Museum and serves as an annex to the Riley Home.

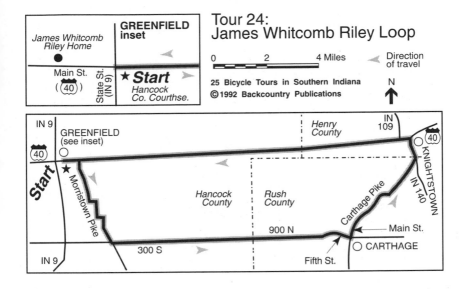

The Hancock County Courthouse was finished in 1898 at a cost of over $262,000. Built of Bedford limestone, it features architectural elements in the Gothic and Romanesque styles. At the north end of the courthouse square is a bronze statue of James Whitcomb Riley. Completed in 1918 by sculptress Myra Richards of Indianapolis, the statue was funded by schoolchildren who ordered mementos from the local art association.

Just west of Greenfield is the Eli Lilly and Company Laboratories. The largest employer in Greenfield, these laboratories include seventy buildings housed on more than 800 acres.

The rooster, original symbol of the Democratic Party, has its origins in Greenfield. A marker at Riley Park denotes Greenfield as the birthplace of this political symbol.

0.0   **START at the Hancock County Courthouse.**

0.0   **RIGHT on Main Street (US 40).**

0.6   **RIGHT on Morristown Pike.**

Morristown Pike is at the eastern edge of James Whitcomb Riley Memorial Park. This 100-acre park contains the Old Log Jail Museum that served as the county jail during the mid-nineteenth century. The road makes several jogs, so be sure to follow the road signs.

3.9   **LEFT on 300S.**

The road becomes 900N in Rush County. 900N becomes Fifth

Statue of James Whitcomb Riley in front of the Hancock County Courthouse

Street at Carthage (which has a convenience store and grocery).
Carthage was settled in 1834 by Quakers from North Carolina. It was named for the community they had left in North Carolina. Be sure to see the Henley Memorial Library on Main Street. It was built in 1902 and has a carving above the door of founder Henry Henley.

12.3   LEFT on Main Street in Carthage.

Main Street becomes Carthage Pike outside Carthage.

16.1   LEFT on IN 140, and follow it into Knightstown (which has convenience stores, grocery stores,s and restaurants).

Knightstown, like Madison, is exceptional in the quality and quantity of its preserved and restored homes and buildings. The community takes great pride in its heritage. Knightstown was platted in 1827 and was named for the chief surveyor of the National Road, Jonathan Knight. The community's economy was closely tied to the commerce of the National Road. As the importance of the National Road waned, Knightstown came to serve agriculture in the area and is also a bedroom community to Indianapolis.

16.9   LEFT on US 40 and follow it to Greenfield.

28.6   RETURN to the Greenfield Square.

Bicycle Repair Service
Greenfield Cycle Inc., 28 North State Street, Greenfield, IN 46140 (317) 462-6525.

25

New Castle - Richmond: Weekender

First half (New Castle to Richmond): 42 miles; easy to moderate
Second half Richmond to New Castle): 28 miles; easy
Both in one day: 70 miles; moderate to easy

This tour includes the Levi Coffin house (on the Underground Railroad); Earlham College; a town that may have been named because of a giant mud hole; the site of the first women's suffrage group in Indiana; the National Road; and Richmond, with a large Quaker population that was credited with the defeat of presidential candidate Henry Clay in the 1844 election and that was instrumental in the Underground Railroad.

The terrain is flat to gently rolling, except for a three-mile section of short, choppy hills on the first half of the loop. You can split it into two days, or do it all in one day.

The tour begins at the Henry County Courthouse in the middle of New Castle, just ten minutes north of Interstate 70 on IN 3. Public parking is available behind the stations or across the street.

0.0 **RIGHT on Main Street.**

0.2 **LEFT on Broad Street. Caution: Traffic may be heavy.**

0.9 **LEFT on 21st Street.**

1.1 **RIGHT on Spring Street.**

1.4 **BEAR LEFT on Brown Road, and follow it out of New Castle.**
Brown Road will become 100N outside of New Castle.

7.6 **LEFT on Wilbur Wright Road.**

8.4 **RIGHT on 200N.**

8.8 **RIGHT on 750E, and follow it to the Wilbur Wright Memorial.**
After viewing the memorial, backtrack to 200N.

9.9 **RIGHT on 200N.**
200N becomes Lamar Road when you enter Wayne County.

14.1 **RIGHT on Old State Road 1.**
Note that Old State Road 1 is the first State Road 1 that you come to.

22.1   LEFT on Oler Road, and follow it into Williamsburg.
This town was laid out in 1830 and, in a sheer stroke of creativity, was named for William Johnson, who platted the town.

29.9   LEFT on Centerville Road in Williamsburg, and follow it to the edge of town.
There are several small groceries, including one that serves sandwiches and ice cream.

30.5   RIGHT on Fountain City Pike, just after crossing some railroad tracks at the edge of Williamsburg.
Follow this road to Fountain City. Fountain City, a Friends settlement, was founded in 1818. Originally called Garden City, its name was changed to Newport in 1834. It took its present name in 1878 after some fountain wells in the community.

34.9   LEFT on US 27, to go to the Levi Coffin house.
The house is on the right (east) side of the road.

35.7   SOUTH (left) on US 27 from Fountain City.

35.8   RIGHT on New Garden Road.

36.5   LEFT at the first intersection (Y) onto East Creek Road.

37.1   RIGHT on Wallace Road (also called Williams Plain Road).

37.1   IMMEDIATE LEFT, back onto East Creek Road.

37.4   LEFT on Pleasant Road.

38.6   RIGHT at the first intersection, onto Flatley Road.

39.3   LEFT on Webster Road.

42.4   RIGHT (south) on Union Pike Road.
Follow this into Richmond. Here the road forks and becomes Fifth N.W. Street. Traffic may be heavy. Follow Fifth N.W. Street to Main Street (US 40). Most of the motels and places of interest are on the east edge of town. Earlham College is 0.5 west of this intersection.

Richmond
Richmond's abundant history is based solely on transportation. As the seat of Wayne County, it is the hub of most of the agricultural and industrial activity in east-central Indiana. Soldiers from George Rogers Clark's Revolutionary War "army" and Friends were the first settlers in the Wayne County area, arriving at the start of the nineteenth century. A meeting of the Society of Friends was established in what is now Richmond in 1807. The Friends' beliefs in pacifism and the equality of all humans was in direct contrast to the racist attitudes of many of the early settlers.

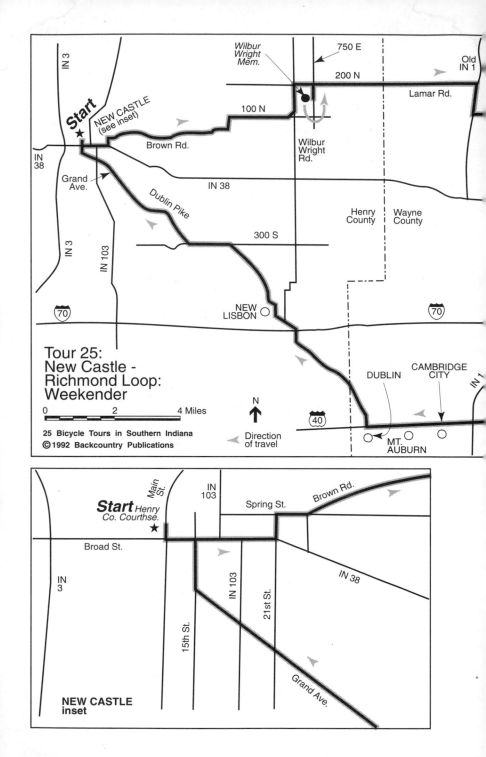

Tour 25:
New Castle -
Richmond Loop:
Weekender

0   2   4 Miles

25 Bicycle Tours in Southern Indiana
©1992 Backcountry Publications

N

↖ Direction
of travel

**NEW CASTLE
inset**

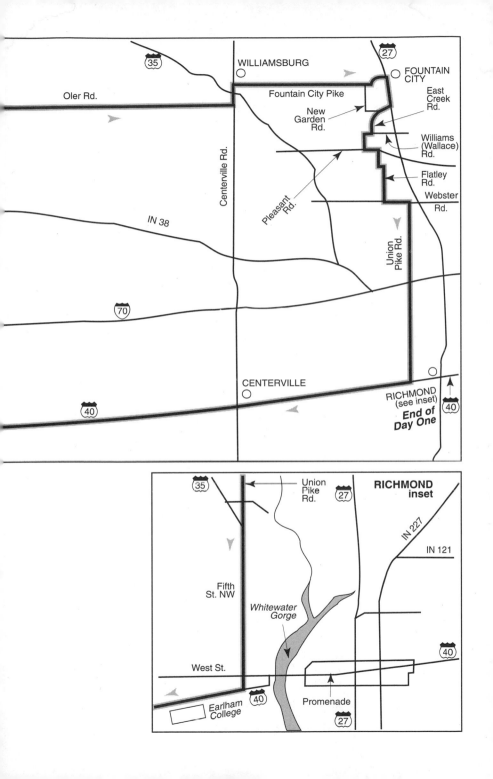

The town was platted in 1816 and was originally called Smithville after proprietor John Smith. In 1818, Jeremiah Cox laid out the town of Coxville, right beside Smithville. Later that same year, the two boys got smart enough to join the two towns into one. They decided that Richmond sounded better than Smith-Coxville or Cox-Smithville. The name Richmond was chosen from several suggestions to describe the richness of the soil in the area. Richmond was incorporated in 1819, when it boasted a population of 350.

In 1827, Richmond was selected as the eastern terminus of the National Road by surveyor Jonathon Knight. The trickle of pioneers heading westward on the road became a torrent that contributed mightily to the purses of the local populace. Richmond's large Friends population has been credited with the defeat of Henry Clay in the 1844 presidential election. At the close of a campaign speech here in October 1842, Clay was handed a petition signed by two thousand local Friends demanding that he free his slaves. Clay's mocking dismissal of the petition and its signers became a national issue that haunted him through the rest of his losing campaign.

Richmond was briefly involved in the doomed flurry of canal-building in the state, but eventually it became a railroad hub for the eastern part of Indiana. The city's railroad activities enabled it to expand and diversify its industrial base rapidly. Like many other Indiana cities, Richmond manufactured a number of early automobiles, including the Richmond Steam Runabout, Davis, Rodefeld, Pilot, and the Wescott. Present Richmond industries range from auto-related companies to the largest producer of greenhouse cut-flowers, Hill Floral Products.

A dozen of these companies employ a hundred people or more each. In April 1969 a massive black gunpowder and natural gas explosion destroyed the downtown shopping district. More than forty people were killed. Out of this devastation the people of Richmond built a new business district and completely redesigned the middle of the city. An outdoor mall has replaced the destroyed area, and all the streets that originally ran through the area have been closed or rebuilt around it. The effect is a very casual, relaxing environment in the middle of a busy town.

If you want to really enjoy Richmond and the Wayne County area, be sure to contact the Chamber of Commerce. The Chamber is very helpful and will give you all the information you need to have fun in Richmond. The area's annual festivals include the Old English May Day (May); the Richmond Area Rose Festival (June); and Pioneer Days (September).

0.0   START the second day of the tour on US 40.

0.0   WEST on US 40 out of Richmond.

Huddleston Museum

Continue through Centerville, Pershing, Cambridge City, and Mt. Auburn/Dublin.

15.2   ENTER Pershing.

Pershing was established in 1827 and was named Georgetown, after local merchant George Shortridge. After an influx of German settlers from Pennsylvania, its name was changed to Germantown. Since there already was a Germantown in the state, the local post office was called East Germantown. In 1918, the anti-German attitudes of World War I resulted in the town's name being changed to Pershing, in honor of General John J. Pershing.

Dublin was platted in 1830. A local anecdote describes the area as having been a giant mudhole, where stagecoaches and wagons had to double-team to get through-hence the name. Another local legend says the town's name came from the Huddleston House, which used to be called the Double Inn because of its double doors. The first women's suffrage group in Indiana, the Women's Rights Society, was organized by Amanda Way in Dublin in 1851. That same year, the society filed a petition with the state General Assembly for voting privileges. The petition was ignored, supposedly because of the onset of the Civil War (ten years later), until the ratification of the Nineteenth Amendment in 1919.

25.9   RIGHT on Dublin Pike in Dublin.

Dublin Pike is the intersection with the stoplight. In New Lisbon, Dublin Pike jogs right onto Wilbur Wright Road for about 50 feet, then back left off of Wilbur Wright Road. In New Castle, Dublin Pike becomes Grand Avenue.

26.7   RIGHT on 15th Street.

27.1   LEFT on Broad Street.

27.3   RIGHT on Main Street, and return to the starting point.

Bicycle Repair Services

Allen's Bike Shop, 300 North 4th Street, Centerville, IN 47330 (317) 855-2332.

Barr's Cycle Sales & Service, 534 North Memorial Drive (State Road 3), New Castle, IN 47362 (317) 529-7200.

Ike's Bikes, 111 South 6th, Richmond, IN 47374 (317) 962-5480.

Appendix

Area Bike Shops not Listed in Tours

A-1 Cyclery
6847 West Washington
Indianapolis, IN 46241
(317) 241-4660

A-1 Cyclery
4150 Lafayette Road
Indianapolis, IN 46254
(317) 291-4462

B & B Campus Bike Shop
508 North McKinley Avenue
Muncie, IN 47303
(317) 282-6389

B & K Bike Shop
112 East Washington
Winchester, IN 47394
(317) 584-2453

Best Bicycle
4012 East 10th
Bloomington, IN 47408
(812) 336-2724

Bickel's Bicycle Shop
21 West 8th Street
Anderson, IN 46016
(317) 649-4341

Bicycle Art
5178 West Pike Plaza
Indianapolis, IN 46254
(317) 297-8687

Bicycle Doctor
8551 West Gardner Road
Bloomington, IN 47403
(812) 825-5050

Bicycle Garage
8354 Castleton Corner Drive
Indianapolis, IN 46250
(317) 842-4140

Bicycle Garage Inc.
507 East Kirkwood Avenue
Bloomington, IN 47408
(812) 339-3457

Bicycle Hospital
3702 Northwestern Avenue
Indianapolis, IN 46208
(317)926-1641

Bicycle Hospital North
9840 North Michigan Road
Carmel, IN 46032
(317) 872-8356

Bicycle Outfitters
7117 North Keystone Avenue
Indianapolis, IN 46240
(317) 251-7800

Bicycle World
715 John Street
Anderson, IN
317-649-4341

Bicycles N'More
209 East High Street
Moorsville, IN 46158
(317) 831-9933

Bike Shack
2703 South Macedonia Avenue
Muncie, IN 47302
(317) 288-3158

Bike Shop
1203 Lincoln Avenue
Connersville, IN 47331
(317) 825-8458

Bike Shop Inc.
1705 East 52nd
Indianpolis, IN 46205
(317) 253-6100

Bike Smith
112 South College Avenue
Bloomington, IN 47403
(812) 339-9970

Billes Schwinn Cyclery
200-D South Greenriver Road
Evansville, IN 47715
(812) 477-8828

Bill's Bicycle Store
20 East Main
Washington, IN 47501
(812) 254-4787

Block's Bicycle Service
7159 East 46th #C
Indianapolis, IN 46226
(317) 547-4313

Bloomington Cyclery
2530 East 10th Street
Bloomington, IN 47408
(812) 336-0241

Carmel Schwinn Cycling & Fitness
912 South Range Line Road
Carmel, IN 46032
(317) 848-1996

Carmel Schwinn Store
510 South Range Line Road
Carmel, IN 46032
(317) 844-7317

Chico's Bicycle Shop
7872 North Michigan Road
Indianapolis, IN 46268
(317) 879-0822

Cycle Enterprizes
1105 East Thompson Road
Indianapolis, IN 46227
(317) 783-5111

Cyclesport
8500 US Route 31 South
1551 Stop 12 #F
Indianapolis, IN 46227
(317) 885-7194

Greenwood Schwinn Cyclery
240 South US Highway 31
Greenwood, IN 46142
(317) 881-8893

Happy Handlebars Bike Shop
9423 E. Washington Street
Indianapolis, IN 46229
(317) 899-4455

Hoffman Bicycle Center
406 South Chestnut
Huntingburg, IN 47542
(812) 683-2014

Jimmy Jim's Bike Shop
963 North Main
Sullivan, IN 47882
(812) 268-6667

Kathy's Schwinn Cycle
5107 Columbus Avenue
Anderson, IN 46013
(317) 644-0230

Kirk's Bike Shop
3304 North Janney Avenue
Muncie, IN 47304
(317) 282-4121

Mac's Bicycle Shop Inc.
815 East Westfield Boulevard
Indianapolis, IN 46220
(317) 257-3349

Matthew's Bicycle Mart
7272 Pendleton Pike
Indianapolis, IN 46226
(317) 547-3456

Rem Bicycle
PO Box 302
Jasper, IN 47547
(812) 634-1454

Smith's Cycle Service
2516 Main
Anderson, IN 46014
(317) 644-4100

Supreme Bicycle Store
5506 Madison Avenue
Indianapolis, IN 46227
(317) 786-9244

Supreme Bicycle Store
37 East Washington
Shelbyville, IN 46176
(317) 398-6907

The Bike Line
6520 Cornell Avenue
Indianapolis, IN 46220
(317) 253-2611

Thorne's Bedford Bicycle
3211 Highway 37 South
Bedford, IN 47421
(812) 275-4656

Tom Lantz Bicycle Center
2715 North Post Road
Indianapolis, IN 46219
(317) 899-1130

Webster's Sporting Goods
8126 Castle Way Court, West
Indianpolis IN 46250
(317) 849-3488

West Side Bicycle Mart
3033 Lafayette Road
Indianapolis, IN 46222
(317) 923-8257

Also from Backcountry Publications and Countryman Press

Backcountry Publications and Countryman Press, long known for fine books on travel and outdoor recreation, offer a range of practical and readable guides. These carefully prepared books feature detailed trail and tour directions, notes on points of interest and natural highlights, maps, and photographs.

Biking Series
25 Bicycle Tours on Delmarva, $9.95
25 Bicycle Tours in the Finger Lakes, Second Edition $9.95
20 Bicycle Tours in the Five Boroughs (New York City), $8.95
25 Bicycle Tours in the Hudson Valley, $9.95
25 Bicycle Tours in Southern Indiana, $10.95
25 Bicycle Tours in Maine, Second Edition $9.95
30 Bicycle Tours in New Hampshire, Third Edition $10.95
25 Bicycle Tours in New Jersey, $9.95
20 Bicycle Tours in and around New York City, $7.95
25 Bicycle Tours in Ohio's Western Reserve, $11.95
25 Bicycle Tours in Eastern Pennsylvania, Second Edition $8.95
25 Bicycle Tours in Vermont, Second Edition $9.95
25 Bicycle Tours in and around Washington, D.C., $9.95
25 Mountain Bike Tours in Massachusetts, $9.95
25 Mountain Bike Tours in Vermont, $9.95

A sampling of other guides
Fifty Hikes in Lower Michigan, $12.95
Fifty Hikes in Ohio, $12.95
Fifty Hikes in Western Pennsylvania, Second Edition $11.95

Our travel and outdoor recreation guides are available through bookstores and specialty shops, or they may be ordered directly from the publisher. To order or request a free catalog write: The Countryman Press, Inc., Dept. APB, PO Box 175, Woodstock, VT 05091. When ordering by mail, please add $2.50 per order for shipping and handling.